"... An important addition to the literature of trauma psychology, shining a beacon of hope for transformation and healing."
From the Foreword by Edward Tick, PhD, author, *War and the Soul*

Thirty Days with My Father

Finding Peace from Wartime PTSD

Christal Presley, PhD

"An incredible memoir ... an important part of the still unhealed wounds of war."
—Nikki Giovanni, a world-renowned poet, writer, and activist

Praise for
Thirty Days with My Father

"Christal Presley is uniquely equipped to tell a tale that affects not only her generation, but that must be understood if we are to prevent second generation PTSD in the sons and daughters of our current wave of returning veterans. Whether you are a professional who treats veterans and their loved ones, or a person at risk for military PTSD, or anyone who cares, you will be profoundly moved by this eloquent, true memoir."

—**Frank M. Ochberg**, MD, Clinical Professor of Psychiatry, Michigan State University; Recipient of the Lifetime Achievement Award of the International Society for Traumatic Stress Studies

"An incredible memoir. I think *Thirty Days with My Father* is an important part of the still unhealed wounds of wars. Christal has given as much of her heart to this story as her father gave to his country. This is not a journey to miss."

—**Nikki Giovanni**, world-renowned poet, writer, and activist

"*Thirty Days with My Father* is an unforgettable account of a daughter struggling to find connection with herself and her father in the aftermath of war. Christal Presley's memoir is a truly inspiring portrayal of survival, forgiveness, and love."

—**Jessica Handler**, author of *Invisible Sisters: A Memoir*

"*Thirty Days with My Father* uses memory and flashback to create a riveting and ultimately loving account of a child terribly affected by her Vietnam veteran father's PTSD. This intergenerational trauma threatens to break the bonds between father and daughter. However, with great courage to face the darkness and great love to heal the wounds, this book is also a journey toward joy—and how a daughter and her father finally find their way back to each other."

—**Louise Nayer**, author of *Burned*

"*Thirty Days with My Father* is close-up and personal, one daughter's attempt to break through her father's post-traumatic stress disorder following Vietnam. It is also a big, big story which affects many Americans—not only soldiers and veterans, as Christal Presley makes clear, but also their entire families, especially the children. *Thirty Days with My Father* is a beautifully written, necessary book— heartrending and affirming all at once."

—**Lee Smith**, bestselling and award-winning author of *Mrs. Darcy Meets the Blue-Eyed Stranger* and *The Last Girls*

THIRTY DAYS WITH MY FATHER

Finding Peace from Wartime PTSD

Christal Presley, PhD

Health Communications, Inc.
Deerfield Beach, Florida

www.hcibooks.com

Library of Congress Cataloging-in-Publication Data

Presley, Christal.
    Thirty days with my father : finding peace from wartime PTSD / Christal Presley.
      p. cm.
    ISBN 978-0-7573-1646-3 (pbk.)
    ISBN 0-7573-1646-8 (pbk.)
    ISBN 978-0-7573-1647-0 (ebook)
    ISBN 0-7573-1647-6 (ebook)
      1. Presley, Christal.   2. Presley, Delmer.   3. Post-traumatic stress disorder.
    4. Vietnam War, 1961–1975—Psychological aspects.   I. Title.
    II. Title: 30 days with my father.
    RC552.P67P72 2012
    616.85'21—dc23

                                                    2012020701

HCI, its logos, and marks are trademarks of Health Communications, Inc.

Publisher: Health Communications, Inc.
           3201 S.W. 15th Street
           Deerfield Beach, FL 33442–8190

Cover design by Larissa Hise Henoch
Interior design and formatting by Lawna Patterson Oldfield

For you,
Dad

Author's Note

This book is based on conversations I had with my father, most of which I recorded by hand. To the best of my ability, I have retained the language and content of those conversations with accuracy. Scenes from my childhood are, of necessity, drawn from memory—the most imperfect recorder of all. Most of the names in this book have been changed.

At that moment of realization
I knew that I had been blind because
I had wished not to see.

—Ernst Toller

Contents

Foreword xi

Prologue xvii

The Thirty-Day Project 1

Day One 7

Day Two 16

Day Three 25

Day Four 30

Day Five 46

Day Six 52

Day Seven 56

Day Eight 62

Day Nine 68

Day Ten 79

Day Eleven 86

Day Twelve 92

Day Thirteen 104

Day Fourteen 108

Day Fifteen 116

Day Sixteen 123

Day Seventeen 135

Day Eighteen 142

Day Nineteen 147

Day Twenty 159

Day Twenty-One 170

Day Twenty-Two 176

Day Twenty-Three 181

Day Twenty-Four 187

Day Twenty-Five 194

Day Twenty-Six 200

Day Twenty-Seven 205

Day Twenty-Eight 211

Day Twenty-Nine 222

Day Thirty 229

After the Thirty Days 233

Epilogue 236

Where Were You? 240

My Wounds Are Not for You to See 242

PTSD Resources 244

Acknowledgments 245

Foreword

Christal Presley's story, which you are about to read, is as old as Greek mythology and as recent as this morning's news.

A father goes to war. He comes home a tortured and wounded soul. He and his family suffer for decades. His child grows up angry, confused, with a deep emptiness. It rots into symptoms and hatred. The wound must be healed. The child goes on a search for the missing father. . . .

We think of Telemachus, son of Odysseus, the Greek warrior-king. Homer's *Odyssey*, our greatest epic of the journey home from war, opens with the veteran's child impelled to search for the father still missing long after the war's end.

Christal Presley is living this story, this time as a daughter of the modern war in Vietnam rather than as a son of the ancient one in Troy. *Thirty Days with My Father* tells her journey through the past and present as she seeks to understand and heal her wounds caused by growing up in a household permeated with war pain. Christal vividly and courageously portrays how lost, hurting, self-punishing, and despairing a veteran's child can become. From nightmares to isolation, from school problems to scab picking, she holds nothing back. We are shown the full and tragic impact of a father's traumatic war wounding on a sensitive growing child. We are reminded once again—when one person goes to war, nobody in that person's circle escapes wounding, either during service or after.

This story is also as old as the Bible.

A child rejects his family and goes wandering in the world, indulging, carousing, and avoiding. But he cannot mature or silence his inner pain; life will not unfold well without reconciliation. Eventually the child turns back toward the waiting father he had scorned.

Christal Presley is also a modern prodigal child, this time a daughter terrified of returning to a home ruled by war trauma. Home nestles in the valleys and back roads of rural America. Christal shows us how and why so many children of veterans become prodigals. She wanders far from the family in her attempts to escape its pain, explosiveness, unpredictability, and silence. *Thirty Days with My Father* vividly portrays this remote and secret world of America's rural traumatized veterans and their families suffering in silence and confusion.

Life Without Father, life lived through the father wound, cannot be complete. We cannot grow into health and wholeness missing an inner positive and reconciled father figure. Like the mythic figures, Christal arrived at a dead end trying to avoid her wounds, trying to move on in the present without completing the past. She decides to take her medicine.

The simplest medicine is often the most effective—and the most terrifying. Unlike Telemachus and the Prodigal, Christal does not have to travel to far lands. Through conversations and journaling, and with the support of a therapist, Christal goes on a quest. It is to talk and listen to her father every day for thirty days in a row. No matter how frightened—just talk. During these conversations she finally breaks the family silence about the war and what it did to them. Along the way she constantly holds the past and present up as mirrors to reflect each other. She restores relationships, digs up and examines her and her father's histories, speaks her truth, and listens with respect to his.

This is always the spiritual task—step into the maelstrom that wounded us. Overcome our terror. Speak our truth. Witness the other's truth. Complete our story. Transform our demons into our angels. Let the past become the past, not because we have fled but because we have tended its wounds, completed it, and let it go. Become new.

In *Thirty Days with My Father,* Christal has given us a moving, fast-paced, well-crafted, and hope-filled modern rendition of these ancient tales. Her story shows how deeply we live the old tales. It indicates, by its ordinariness and our awareness of the millions of Americans who have served in wars, how very many millions of people suffer this same story. But Christal does not merely suffer her fate. She models how passionately we must live our stories and seek their hidden treasures. Ultimately she shines a beacon of hope for the transformation and healing that is possible when we do.

Christal did not set out to retell old myths. She is just living them, which makes them honest and real. She is far more conscious of the degree to which millions of veterans are suffering traumatic wounding and millions of their children are suffering the transgenerational consequences that can scar them for life. Thus *Thirty Days with My Father* is an important addition to the literature of trauma psychology. Many veterans and their family members will read this book and say, "Me, too!" Many will see that they are not crazy but their wounds are characteristic. Many will affirm that war goes on and on, as long as it remains silent and closeted, wounding through the generations. Many in the public who have not served and do not know will be moved to tears by Christal's story and better understand the invisible wounding of war and how many families suffer from it in silence and secret.

Christal is on the cutting edge of war healing in a number of ways. She helps open the field of trauma studies by giving testimony to the little-examined focus on the suffering of survivors' children. She helps explain some confusing childhood troubles by exposing their source. She shows the family origins of our psychological turmoil. She breaks the silence about war's long and terrible aftereffects that afflict our entire society. She organizes other children of veterans to reach out, overcome isolation, find each other, and tell their stories. In this way her wound has propelled her into activism. She is founder of United Children of Veterans, website: www.unitedchildrenof veterans.com. And she achieves and models profound healing for herself and her entire family through the most direct of human means and tools. Christal listens to the honest message of her wounds, then with love and courage turns back to her missing father. Then they just talk and listen with open hearts and welcoming, nonjudgmental attitudes. She uses a human path to heal and it works.

Christal's book ends with her visit to Vietnam. There she finally stood on the very ground on which her father fought and was wounded in spirit. There she literally and spiritually stepped into his footprints and walked as one with him.

Marble Mountain, outside Da Nang, is an ancient sacred mountain hewed and shaped into temples and statues scattered among rocky walkways. It was a Viet Cong field hospital and site of brutal combat during the war. Before and since, it is a place that radiates peace and beauty.

These words of the Buddha are scripted on a sign before one of the mountain temples:

Hatreds never cease

By hatreds in this world.

By love they cease.

This is an ancient law.

Christal Presley had hated her past, her father, herself, and her own lot and destiny. She finally brought love, courage, and open-heartedness to all of these. Then love and forgiveness bloomed, and the prodigal child returned home to the father's loving embrace. Then father and daughter were reunited, what war sundered was restored, and the path was marked for others to follow.

The most fitting words to close this introduction to the story you will now read, and to remember always as a spiritual dictum we can all believe in, are the ones Christal borrows from the famous playwright Tennessee Williams: "The violets in the mountains have broken the rocks."

Edward Tick, PhD
Author, *War and the Soul*
Founding Co-Director, Soldier's Heart

Prologue

*I*n my dreams, we have a different life.

My father, young and fit, runs on the beach with a Frisbee. His dark hair is tousled, his skin aglow with tanning oil. Waves crash behind him. It is a hot summer afternoon with a slight breeze that keeps it from being totally oppressive. His feet leave wet prints in the sand along the water's edge.

I stretch my legs to reach the exact places he has touched, to put my feet inside the imprints of his. With all my might, I try to catch him.

In this dream, my mother relaxes in a chaise lounge beneath an umbrella. She sips a soda and looks up over her sunglasses to check on us from time to time. She smiles and waves, then goes back to reading her magazine about flowers. It is hard to decide what color rosebushes she should plant around our mailbox. This is her biggest worry.

Overhead, seagulls hang in midair above the waves. Music from someone's boom box plays in the background. It is a light and airy tune that makes me want to dance. I do.

In this fantasy, my mother will get in the water before long. We all will—the three of us. We will swim just beyond the waves and laugh as the warm water laps against our necks. We are not afraid.

Even when we are in over our heads, when our feet no longer reach the thick sand underwater, we swim fast and strong. We have no doubts we will get back to the shore. If one of us gets pulled out by the current, another of us will reel that person back in.

This is a safe place, a place where we have come many times. It is a treasured late summer vacation just before school starts again. Tired and happy, gritty with sand and salt, hand in hand, we walk back to our hotel room.

In my dream, we fish for crabs in the evening. We tie raw squid in our baskets and heave them over the side of the pier. I catch more than anyone else.

We throw most of the crabs back and cook the rest that same night right on the beach. My father throws them live into a big pot of boiling water set over a fire he's made. I walk on the beach and look for sea-shells as the sun sets.

Back in our hotel room, I am stuffed to the brim and sleepy-eyed. My father rubs aloe on my burned shoulders. He kisses me on my forehead and tucks me into bed. My mother reads me a story and lies beside me until I can barely keep my eyes open. They laugh and whisper in the darkness, holding each other close in the bed next to mine as I drift into sleep.

In my dreams, my family is whole. In my dreams, there was no war.

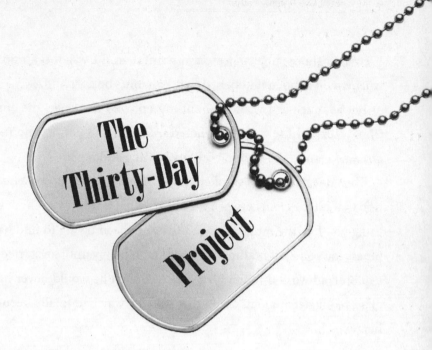

The Thirty-Day Project

"**D**ad says he'll do it," my mother tells me.

My hand is suddenly sweaty as I press the phone against my ear. Two days earlier, I'd called my mother to ask if she would relay a request to my father. I'd decided that would be the best way to gauge his reaction without actually having to deal with him directly. I wanted to know if he would be okay with me calling him every day for thirty days to ask him about his experiences during the Vietnam War for a writing project.

I had been writing about my life for years to work through some emotional issues, leaving out anything related to my father or to

Vietnam. Those subjects were too painful, and I was too afraid of what would happen if I opened that Pandora's box.

But as much as I wrote—about my botched marriage, the emotional turmoil I felt, and my failed quest to find contentment—I remained stuck. Blocked in both my writing and my life.

Then one day a guest speaker at a writing workshop posed a question that hit me right between the eyes: "What if you wrote about the thing you fear the most?" He said that he'd been trying to find happiness for years but nothing had made him happy until he started to explore and work through his fears. Although he would never have expected it starting out, doing that was the way he'd finally become happy.

Frightening as it was, the idea also intrigued me. Could the key to finding happiness really be so simple? Nothing else I'd done had made me feel fulfilled, and I was tired of being miserable. I was willing to try just about anything.

I knew exactly what I feared the most: my father and the war he had brought home with him from Vietnam. But that was the last thing I wanted to write about. I'd spent the last thirteen years of my life trying to put Vietnam behind me, and I'd gotten pretty good at pretending to be happy. But on some level I must have known that I wouldn't ever be truly happy until I addressed all the unspoken questions and issues with my father that I'd been trying so hard to ignore. Until then, I'd be stuck—not only in my writing, but in my life.

When I asked my mother to ask him, I thought I was finally strong enough to go through with it and hear whatever he had to say. But when he agreed, I realized that my initial bravado had been resting precariously on my deep-down certainty that my father would never say yes. He wasn't *supposed* to say yes. Although I hadn't been consciously aware of it when I made the call to my mother, I must have subconsciously believed that when he refused I'd be able to tell myself I'd tried and go right on being angry with him as I had for as long as I could remember.

But he said yes. Now what?

Too late to back out now. I'd just have to figure it out along the way.

• • •

The following morning I decided to go back into therapy for the first time in two years—just for a month, in case I needed some support to get me through the next thirty days. I thought I'd been doing very well. But what if the plan I'd come up with to move me forward actually wound up setting me back? I didn't want that to happen. I needed to stay strong.

The therapist I found, Dr. Louise James, was older than I expected, old enough to be my mother. As she read through the lengthy questionnaire I had just completed, I sat across from her, silently counting the framed photographs adorning the walls and then the potted plants scattered about the office.

I've always hated the first appointment with a new therapist, and there have been many. By the time I went to see Dr. James, I was highly skilled at sizing them up. I could tell right away if someone would be able to help me. Or if it was someone whom I *wanted* to help me. I liked Dr. James. Her voice was kind, and she didn't try to impress me with her qualifications.

As ridiculous as it now sounds even to me, I remember clearly the first thing I said when I walked through the door of her tidy, homey office: "I've had more therapists than I can remember. I'm not here to begin therapy again. I only need you for thirty days because I'm doing this project with my dad. Once a week for thirty days; that's all I need." That's how I thought of it—as a project. Like a school assignment I'd complete, hand in, then file it away and be done.

Dr. James wrote down everything I said without ever taking her eyes off mine. She didn't even glance at her paper. You have to admire talent like that.

She must have been doubtful (and who could blame her?) because the first thing she told me was, "I will only be here until February. After that, I'm retiring. You might want to go with someone else. Someone who will be here longer."

I kept assuring her that wouldn't be a problem. It was only November. My thirty-day plan meant I'd be out of there before Christmas. Finally she just shrugged.

"So you say your father has posttraumatic stress disorder, and there were times when you were growing up that you didn't speak to each other for days, even weeks on end?" she asked. "But he and your mother are still together, and you lived with them until you were eighteen, correct?"

Her questions stung. I knew that my relationship with my father was broken, but hearing those words spoken aloud somehow made it seem that much worse. I nodded.

"And now you're going to talk to him every day for the next month to try to get to know him?"

I took a deep breath. "Yes," I replied.

"When was he diagnosed?" she wanted to know.

I shrugged my shoulders. "I was in elementary school," I muttered, staring down at my lap. Just thinking about that time in my life makes me nervous. "He's had symptoms since I was five, maybe longer."

"And you say you, too, have been diagnosed with PTSD. When did you start having symptoms?"

"I don't remember," I said. "Around that same time maybe."

I always knew there was something wrong with me, but it wasn't until I went to a therapist when I was in college that anyone had put a name to my problems. Although there's no "official" illness known as intergenerational PTSD, it is well known and acknowledged that the children of veterans with PTSD may develop symptoms of their own that are related to dealing with their parent's symptoms, and this is sometimes called "secondary traumatization."

"What are your parents' names?" Dr. James asked.

I looked down. "Delmer and Judy Presley," I said tentatively, not quite sure why she needed to know this.

"Okay," she said. "If we're going to do this together, I want you to start a journal. Write down all the things you feel angry about. What your conversations bring up for you. What you remember, and how it felt for you as a child. Do you feel angry right now?"

Did I feel angry right now? I didn't know. I thought I was past that. Did I *sound* angry?

I handed Dr. James my co-pay and closed the door behind me. My mind was already churning. I'd agreed to keep the journal, but where would I start? It had been twenty-six years since I first realized something about my family was horribly, terribly wrong. Twenty-six years that I'd been hiding from my father.

I was barely out of the building when I was surprised by the words that suddenly flashed through my mind: *Dear world*, I would write. *You missed it. I was dying back then, I couldn't tell you, and you goddamn missed it. . . .*

Day One

I force myself to make the first call.

"You're still doing the project with me, aren't you?" I ask when my dad picks up the phone. I bite my lip. Knowing how difficult this is going to be suddenly feels overwhelming. Would we be able to handle whatever came up? What if I failed? Where would we be then? I almost cry when I hear his voice, but I don't. "It'll just be some questions, Dad," I say, trying to keep my voice light but hearing it tremble in spite of myself.

"Questions about what?" he wants to know. He sounds suspicious.

What's that about? Mom said she'd explained it all to him. We'd do this thirty-day project together, and I'd write down our conversations as we went. I'd always used my writing as a way to process my feelings, and maybe I'd be able to turn our conversations into a book. She said she'd told him that, too.

I hold my breath. "Questions about the war. About *Vietnam*."

That unspeakable word is a cancer in my throat when I say it. It's the word my mother and I only whispered, if we ever dared to speak it at all.

"I don't want to talk about the war," he snaps. "I don't know anything about a war."

I feel as if I've just been slapped in the face.

Even though I had initially hoped—and assumed—that he'd refuse to talk to me, when he said yes, I got my hopes up. Now they are dashed again, and I am flooded with memories of all the sudden, unexplained mood swings he had when I was growing up and of how frightening they were to me.

All I can do is hang up the phone.

Journal

I remember the first time I was afraid of my father.

I was five, home from school and tucked away in my sofa-cushion wolf den watching *Tom & Jerry* reruns. I was eating crackers, dipping them in potted meat, blowing away the crumbs when they fell onto my lap.

We lived in a trailer, in a trailer park called New Garden Estates in Honaker, Virginia. I had a ten-gallon aquarium with a black pop-eyed goldfish inside. I had an orange-and-white cat named Tiger that I pushed around in a wagon. I had two dogs, Smokey and Rusty. My favorite drink was the lemon-lime slush from IGA. My mother had just quilted me a My Little Pony bedspread and purple curtains to match.

Since I clearly remember the day I first became afraid, I know that my dad and my life had once been different, and my mother has the pictures to prove there was some normalcy even after everything changed. But I can't remember much about those times.

"Your father used to hold you," she says, as she points to the pictures of my father and me that she has arranged in a scrapbook. She looks happy when she says it. She really remembers us that way.

It must help to have something to hold onto like that.

On that day when I was five, my father came home from work, his eyes wild and his face unshaven. He was a welder who worked on mining equipment and came home with his clothes black and thick with grit. His habit was to put down his lunchbox, take off his work boots, and strip down to his underclothes as soon as he came in the door. My mom would come in to greet him, put his dirty clothes in a plastic bag, pick up his empty lunchbox, and take them into the kitchen. On this day, however, as he collapsed into the rocking chair in the corner and struggled to untie his boots, his hands trembled and his breathing was labored.

"Daddy?" I whispered.

He did not respond; he didn't even acknowledge I was there.

Something was wrong. This was not my father. Everything about this man seemed unfamiliar to me, from his countenance to his actions. It was as if some supernatural force had invaded my father's body and made him act strange.

My mom came in as usual and helped him back to the kitchen. I hid behind the sofa, knees pressed into the shag carpet, and held my breath as I tried to hear their frantic whispers. At some point, when no one was looking, I escaped to my bedroom and hid in the closet. I did not come out for dinner. I remember clutching a little plastic toy called a Glow Worm that my father had bought me for my birthday that year and peering through the slats of my closet door. The black pop-eyed goldfish gulped for air at the top of its tank.

Back then I had not yet heard of Vietnam, did not yet realize that a war in which I'd never fought would shape the course of my life.

This was the moment it all came undone, and after which it would never go back to normal.

"You are smiling in all the pictures," my mother says, every time I see her. "Look how happy you were."

I don't remember being the girl in those happy photographs, but she's right. It's me looking out from all those pictures, and I *was* smiling. I'm smiling in every single picture my mother put in the scrapbook.

"This is your childhood," she says proudly, pointing to a picture of me when I turned twelve, sitting behind a birthday cake with a horse drawn in icing on the top. She made that cake herself and gave me a whole cup of icing and let me eat it with my fingers because she knew I didn't like the cake part. That's one thing I do remember.

"And here," she says, as she flips the page backward. "Look at you in your pool with Amy. You loved Amy. She was like a sister to you."

In the picture, my neighbor Amy and I are both crammed through the center of the same orange tube, taking up most of the plastic kiddy pool we had in the yard and attempting to float in less than two feet of water. Amy points her finger straight ahead, looking as if she's daring the person with the camera to take the picture.

Eleven years, ten months. June 1990. Christal Presley. Amy Stinson. My mother has neatly written these words beside the picture.

She looks at me closely, trying to gauge my reaction. I want to feel something. Nostalgia. Joy. Something. If I was almost twelve back then, Amy was almost eight. I wish I remembered that day.

"Look at this one," my mother says. I am nine, trying to bounce a basketball on the grass behind our trailer. There's an azalea with pink flowers to my left, a freshly tilled garden to my right. A little bird feeder is attached to the pole on our clothesline. "You used to run through that garden barefooted," she says. "You'd eat Fruity Pebbles while you ran. Do you remember that?"

I nod. This is one of the few good things about my childhood that my brain has not erased.

"The mind is a mysterious thing," one of my first therapists said. "When we block out the trauma, sometimes we block out the good memories, too."

Sometimes, however, it feels as if I kept the trauma and blocked out most of the good things. I am still not convinced my mind works like everyone else's, but if there's one thing I do know, it's that my mother has always loved me. She loved me so much that she erased the devastating effects of the war as best she could, cleaned it all up so I wouldn't be so afraid. But it didn't work. You can't pretend something isn't happening at the same time you're dealing with it on a daily basis. And not talking about it actually makes it seem worse instead of better. When I look at those pictures all I see is the unspoken war and nothing else.

I was a seriously disturbed child, but no one saw it, and if they did, no one mentioned it.

In elementary school, I changed my classmates' answers on tests so that they would not score 100s. Once I stole my neighbor's photograph of a family outing at the beach, cut their heads out of the picture, replaced them with cutouts of my parents and me, and then took the picture to school.

"We went to the beach this weekend," I told everyone, including my teachers, while flashing the picture in their faces. "Just my mother, my father, and me."

Their eyes grew large as they stared blankly at the clumsily doctored picture, cocking their heads to the side in confusion. They nodded, then looked away as fast as they could.

I also faked being sick whenever I could, often holding the thermometer next to the heater to raise the temperature just enough to make it seem like I had a fever. I ate poison ivy and stapled the back of my hand to see what would happen.

When one of my teachers finally called my mother because, she said, she was "worried" about me, my mother took me into my bedroom where, crying and holding her Bible, she warned that unless I was a "good girl" I would never get to heaven.

"We won't ever tell your father what you've done," she said in a whisper, shaking her head. "He couldn't handle it. It might make him even sicker."

That was the first and last conversation she ever had with me about my teacher's concerns. I tried hard to stay off everyone's radar after that, especially because I feared I really would be making my father's condition even worse if he found out what I'd been doing.

But by trying to remain unnoticed I also felt invisible, as if I were in the world but not of it.

I developed a facial tic, my eyebrows dancing oddly up my forehead whenever I spoke.

I did not enjoy the company of others. I preferred to be alone. Put me in a room with people at close quarters, and before long I'd be dying to get out of there.

I liked hiding in my bedroom closet, away from everyone and everything. I'd turn off all the lights so I could read by flashlight.

I had friends, but they did not know me. I didn't want them to.

Leave me alone, and I would be just fine.

Everyone else was unpredictable; I could not trust anyone but myself.

Thank God I had my dogs. I wouldn't have survived without them. We had "outside" dogs back then. Smokey and his son, Rusty, were oversized Pomeranians in black and yellow. They lived in a fenced dog lot in our backyard, in a doghouse my father made himself. Rusty danced in a circle and chased balls but would not return them. Smokey laid down more often than he stood up, preferring to relax in the shade and watch from a distance. I think that one of the reasons I loved them so much is that they were so predictable when so much else in my life seemed to be just the opposite.

They were always loving and happy to see me, and no matter what else was happening, when I was with my dogs, I was fine. I could forget about all the bad when I stroked their heads. I could go to another place when I looked into their gentle brown eyes. Sometimes I slipped out my window at night and sat in the dog lot with them. I was calm when I was there. As long as I had my dogs, I'd be fine, which I think was pretty much how my father felt about his guitar.

When I was seven, my father tried to teach me to play the guitar. I remember sitting on his lap, our arms intertwined, as he pressed my fingers against the strings. I had never realized his hands were so calloused. It was the first time I recall his touching me in a loving way, even though I'm sure there must have been many others before then.

"This is *C*," he said. "Remember *C*."

"*C*," I repeated, although I knew I'd never remember anything except the roughness of his hands.

"Someday you'll be able to tell people you took guitar lessons from the best in the world," he said.

I nodded.

"Ralph Stanley asked me to play with him once," my father said. I could feel his breath against my neck. "Turned him down." I nodded again. "Know why I turned him down?" my father prodded.

Dr. Ralph Stanley lived—and still lives—not far from Honaker, deep in the Clinch Mountains of Appalachia. Way back before his haunting ballad "O Death" was featured in the movie *O Brother, Where Art Thou?* my father was a diehard fan. Years ago, he had sent Stanley some tapes of him playing the guitar, and Stanley was so impressed that he called my father and insisted he come to his house and play with him.

But a blizzard arrived the night my father was supposed to go, and he never rescheduled.

I had heard this story many times, but it never got old. It was easy to pretend I didn't know what was coming next.

"Why didn't you play with Ralph Stanley, Dad?"

We both sank deeper into the chair.

"Because I am the best in the world, and the best in the world doesn't play with just anyone. . . . This is *D*," he continued, pressing my fingers against the thick wires and holding them there. "Could have made it in Nashville," he muttered under his breath, more to himself than to me. "Could have been famous."

My fingers stung when I pulled them away. They had dents in the tips the exact width of the guitar strings. No one had said that learning the guitar was going to hurt.

My father paled, his face gray, as he examined the rawness of my fingers. He turned them over and over in his hands. With a look that was part frown and part fear, he pushed me softly from his lap. I slid to the floor in a heap. I was sure I had done something wrong, even though, looking back, it's much more likely that he was afraid he had hurt me.

He never gave me another guitar lesson after that, no matter how much I begged.

Day Two

I'm afraid to make the call to my father tonight. Afraid of what he'll say—or what he won't. I sit there with the phone in my hand, dreading the emotions that will come either way.

It's why I've stayed away so long, and why I go home only once a year. This year I am going for Christmas. I am always careful to keep my visits brief, never more than two or three days. Pop in. Pop out. Fulfill my duty for the year. Leave before I lose my mind.

I don't like who I am when I'm there. I become jumpy. Irritable. Guilty. I keep remembering the glassy-eyed deer heads that used to be on the living room wall of the trailer my parents no longer live in. Those dead deer eyes witnessed everything, but like my mother, my father, and me, they did not speak about any of it.

"Please come home," my mother cries and begs over and over. "I miss you. I love you."

And still, I don't go.

She doesn't understand.

"Remember how happy you look in the pictures?" she persists, trying to convince me. "You are smiling in every one, such a pretty little girl."

No matter how much I prepare and swear to myself that this visit will be different, year after year, it is always the same. As soon as I pass Abingdon, at the first glimpse of the mountains, I start to feel Vietnam all around me. It almost makes me shudder. For me, the word "Vietnam" has never signified a country or even a foreign war. To me it has always been synonymous with my father and the undeclared war that raged within our home. The jaggedness of those mountains always triggers memories of the secret war that threatens to destroy the bulwark of the life I have carefully constructed for myself. It's as if I've foolishly lifted my head above the rim of my carefully dug foxhole and given the enemy a clear shot.

When I imagine walking through my parents' door, the images in my mind are always the same—I see my father curled in a fetal position on his bed, his back toward me. I also see the tall wooden gun cabinet in the bedroom, my father leaning inside to get the gun with which he's threatened to blow his brains out a thousand times. And I see a little girl who hides in her closet, reading books and writing stories by the light of a flashlight. I try to ward off the darkness of these memories by reminding myself I don't live here anymore. I've moved out of the war zone.

At this point in the journey back home I try to imagine I'm inside a bubble made of thick, impenetrable glass. I take deep breaths, count to ten, and work hard to keep my muscles relaxed.

"You should come home more often," my slews of aunts, uncles, and cousins say, in the brief moments of each year's visit when they see me. "Such a city girl you have become. You stay gone so long. Don't be such a stranger, you hear?"

I look them all dead in the eyes, put on a smile, then breathe a sigh of relief as I walk out the door.

I wonder what it would feel like if they really knew me. If they had asked back then.

If I'd told them the truth.

If I'd felt safe enough to tell.

• • •

I snap out of it and force myself to dial my parents' number, hoping no one picks up. Truth to tell, I really don't expect anyone to answer because I'm calling on a Wednesday evening when I know they go to church. We always went to church three times a week—Sunday morning, Sunday evening, and Wednesday evening.

"Hello?" my father says on the third ring.

I close my eyes.

"Hi, Dad," I say with trepidation. Then, in one big breath, "I called to talk, but something came up just as I dialed your number. I'll call back tomorrow."

I hang up before he can respond.

I don't know if I can do this. I've already wasted two days, and we've exchanged no more than a few words. I'm still angry from the first conversation, and if he's not going to talk about the war, I really don't know what we have to talk about. But if I don't talk to him, how can I ever put the past to rest? Suddenly it seems like I've gotten myself into a no-win situation.

My dogs, Arthur and Duma, seem to sense that something is wrong. They hardly leave my side. Arthur is a cream Afghan hound and so tall he reaches my waist. He used to have long, flowing hair all the way to the floor, but I keep it shaved these days. Duma is a hairless Chinese crested and so tiny he has to jump to reach my knees. I sit on the sofa with Arthur on one side and Duma on the other, their gentle presence more comforting than that of any human I know.

Journal

I was six when my father went to the VA hospital for the first time because he was so emotionally disturbed and his hands shook so badly that he knew he shouldn't go on working and that he needed to qualify for disability insurance. That's when he was finally diagnosed with PTSD, but it would take six years before he was finally approved for full disability. Meanwhile, he just kept on working.

To me, "posttraumatic stress disorder" was just a bunch of words. All I knew was that it had something to do with my dad's brain and he seemed to be going crazy. And I knew it was bad because my mom told me that if anyone found out how sick he was, they'd come and take him away forever—and they'd take me away, too, and she couldn't live like that. If he had to be that sick, I wanted him to have something everybody could understand. So I picked brain cancer.

I envisioned a map of the human brain like I had seen on television.

"Here is a *normal* brain," a doctor in a white lab coat would say solemnly. He would use a pointer to show his audience the parts of the brain displayed on a screen. Each one would light up in a different color as he talked about it.

"Now, here is your *father's* brain," the same doctor would say, shaking his head, as my father's brain appeared on the screen. This one didn't look like the other brain. The doctor could not point out the individual parts. Everything was a jumble of mush and sharp wires all clumped together.

"Nothing we can do about *this* one," he'd say, and move on to the next.

Did my brain look like everyone else's—or was I a freak, too? I wondered.

I was not normal. That was for sure. When I went to school on a Monday and the teacher asked, "How was your weekend?" I couldn't fathom answering that question honestly, the way the other kids did. I felt as if the world I inhabited was different from the one in which everyone else lived.

When my father shut himself in his room for weeks on end or took his gun and went to the river, I made plans to tell everyone at school that he'd died of brain cancer and talk up all the gruesome details. *He'd been fishing,* I planned to tell them. *His brain hadn't been right for a while. Suddenly, it gave out. Just like that. Like when your heart stops beating. His brain stopped working, and he fell right in the water. They found his waterlogged body with his head all bloody washed a mile downstream. He'd hit his head on some rocks. That's why there was so much blood.*

Everyone at school would feel sorry for me if I had a father who died of brain cancer.

My father threatened to kill himself so many times, and the events surrounding each episode were so similar, that it was hard to separate them in my mind. He would already be depressed. Then something would happen—maybe he'd hear a loud booming noise or he'd get a bill he couldn't pay. Maybe the lawn mower would break or the car would get a flat tire. Things that would simply annoy or mildly upset anyone else would be enough to throw him over the edge.

Then, keys jingling in hand, he'd march through the hall toward the bedroom, unlock the gun cabinet, and grab his rifle. He kept it cleaned and loaded, so it was always ready. A man on a mission, his rifle cradled against his chest like an infant and his pupils so dilated you could hardly see the whites of his eyes, he would march back through the house and out the door, but not before uttering a single sentence: "I'm going to the river to kill myself."

We used to try to stop him, but there was no use. I cried and wailed, but to no avail. For a while my mother even threatened to kill herself if he so much as left our property with that gun. But he knew she'd never do it. She wanted to get to heaven, and according to her beliefs there was no quicker way to hell than to commit suicide.

So in the end we just had to let him go. Naturally we were nervous wrecks the entire time he was gone, always imagining the worst. We ate junk food to comfort ourselves and slept huddled together tightly in my bed. We didn't talk about what was happening or how we felt. Instead, we made small talk about my fish, my dogs, or the Bible to fill in all the spaces between the things we did not mention.

And somehow, several hours later, my father always came back.

I never really knew *why* he came back, and I've never asked him. I'd like to believe it was for my basketball and softball games, to strum his guitar on the back porch. I'd like to believe he came back to anchor the roof on our trailer so it wouldn't blow away, to till the ground so my mother could plant flowers, so she could have a garden every year. At the time, however, I actually thought he came back just to torture us some more.

• • •

Shortly after my father went to the VA, the pills started to come in the mail. To me it seemed as if a new shipment arrived every day, but that can't be true. In any case, one of my jobs was to go out to the mailbox, get the pills, and take them into the kitchen where my mother and I lined the bottles up, row by row, in a cabinet already stuffed to the brim with other medicines from the VA. We never really discussed what we were doing. It was just another chore. I helped her string the beans for supper, and I helped her arrange my father's pill bottles in perfect rows.

Around the same time, my mother seemed to become obsessed with death. The local Christian radio station, WGTH–The Sheep, would broadcast obituaries, and they blasted through our house all day long. My mother and I started to attend three or four funerals a week. In our small town we knew (or knew of) most of the people whose funerals we attended. And whether we knew them well or not, we'd often pay sick calls at the hospital or at their homes. Between the sick calls, the funerals, and my father's illness, sickness and death became the predominating constants in our lives.

When my father first started experiencing rage, depression, and suicidal thoughts, I felt really sorry for him and I wanted to do whatever I could to help. I truly believed that if I loved him enough I could make him better. But he didn't allow me to do that. Instead, the sicker he got, the more he locked himself away from me. And the more I realized how powerless I was, the guiltier and angrier I felt. I remember my mother telling me that if we both followed the Bible *exactly* and if I was a good girl, God would heal my father. I tried to do everything I was supposed to, because I felt as if my thoughts and actions were directly related to my father's health and happiness. But no matter how hard I tried, I couldn't be perfect. In our little town where virtually everyone was, and is, a fundamentalist Baptist or a member of the Pentecostal Holiness Church, being perfect was considered the only way to reach heaven, and the family's reputation in the community meant everything. So, I was angry not only at myself but also at my mother, and at God, and then I was also angry at my father, because I started to think that if he really loved me he'd get better and be the normal father I desperately wanted to have.

Even after thirteen years, I still cringe when I think of the Pentecostal Holiness Church. I associate that church with all the worst of my childhood and the pressure of not telling the truth. Inside my parents' home there was no need to pretend my family was happy. But everywhere else—and especially at church—we put on quite a show.

"How is your father?" our pastor would ask when my dad didn't come.

"He's fine," I'd say with a bright, phony smile. I was quite the actress. I used to practice in the mirror, studying which smiles looked real and which looked fake.

"Just fine," my mother would repeat for emphasis. Then she'd grab my hand as if to say, *I'm with you. We can do this.* We never talked about it beforehand, but we always stayed together and stuck to the script.

Truth is, however, there were times when we didn't have to pretend. Sometimes things really were normal. Although these periods seemed few and far between, there were shining moments when we couldn't see the war in my father at all. There were times when he told me stories, times when I sang while he played the guitar, times when the two of us went fishing together. I must remind myself of these good times. They happened—even if I have a hard time remembering them.

Sometimes on Sundays after church, when we drove across Big-A Mountain to see my father's mother, Mamaw Presley, I'd sit and listen to my aunts and uncles tell stories of what my dad was like as a child. He had a pet pigeon named JoJo. He threw rocks in the creek to stir up the snakes. The first time he saw a plane in the sky, he thought the end of the world was at hand.

I could never imagine my father as the child they described. It was as if those stories were about some other person I'd never met.

Several years after seeing that plane, when he was eighteen, my father was drafted and left on one to go across the world to a country he hadn't even known existed, to fight in a war he didn't understand.

His brothers and sisters used to tell each other (when they thought I was out of earshot) that the young man they waved off to war never did come back.

Day Three

The next day I can't work up the courage to dial my parents' number at all. When I finally do call on Friday, I think my father will be at home, but he isn't. I'd forgotten that he and my mother were going to see a play about the Carter family called *Keep on the Sunny Side* at a local theater. It's become a tradition for my parents to go to a play there at about this time every year, which reminds me that my father has shown improvement over the past few years. *He's getting better. Isn't he?*

I'm disappointed he isn't available, yet also relieved.

I don't leave a message. I will see him in person tomorrow. He is driving my mother to Knoxville, Tennessee, which is more or less halfway between my home in Atlanta and theirs. I'll meet them there and bring her back to my place for Thanksgiving. We'd arranged all this a few weeks earlier because, as much as I wanted to see her for the holiday, I was anxious about returning to Virginia.

We're meeting at a gas station, a spot we'd chosen because it wouldn't be too noisy or too crowded and it could be reached without my father having to drive on a major highway. Noise, crowds, highways—any one of these things could trigger an episode of PTSD. My mom isn't really comfortable going too far from home either, but she's willing to take the chance and suffer the discomfort in order to spend time with me.

I don't know whether seeing my father in person will be easier or harder than trying to talk on the phone. It will either be a good way to break the ice and plunge in, or it will torpedo the project before it's really begun. With my father, I never know what to expect. Just about anything could set him off.

Journal

I remember one day when I was eight sitting at the kitchen table with my father on a Saturday morning after my mother had left to work the drive-through at the bank, which was then open a half day on Saturday. He seemed distant and preoccupied, using his fork to push his food into a large pile in the middle of his plate as I sat opposite him in total silence.

Then, somehow, I knocked over a glass of water. I tried my best to catch the glass before it hit the floor and shattered, but it was too late. The noise sent my father into a fury, his eyes wild, bulging, and unblinking.

"I'll clean it up," I said, my voice trembling. "I'm sorry. God, I'm so sorry."

My apology wasn't good enough. He had already been triggered. There was no going back. He came after me without warning, without saying a single word. I ran around the table, turned over a chair in front of him to buy time, ducked to my room, and locked the door.

"You open this door!" he yelled at last, beating at it with thunderous fists. "You open this door or I'll bust it down!"

I pressed my body against my dresser so hard I saw stars, but I managed to push it in front of the door. Then I threw open my closet door, curled up in the far corner, heart pounding from exertion and terror as I watched through the slats and tried to catch my breath.

My father's knuckles cracked against the wood. He was going to kill me, and my mother wasn't there to help. In the past, he'd whipped me with his thick leather belt a few times, with his hands, and once even with a tree limb when he was in one of his rages, but he'd never actually threatened to kill me. Still, I knew how strong he was, and whenever he lost control like that I feared the worst. Who knows, when he was like that he might even kill me without ever meaning to.

Locked in my closet that day, I put my hands over my ears and prayed. I had never felt God in my life, but I prayed because it was the only thing I knew to do. I pressed my hands tighter over my ears, shut my eyes, and hoped that dying wouldn't hurt too much. I began picturing myself standing in front of Jesus Himself. He would make the judgment call, put me on the right or on the left, get out His checklist of all the things I had done wrong, and size me up.

Please forgive me for my sins. Forgive me for my sins, I prayed over and over in my head.

I hoped my prayers would be answered at the exact moment before I died. That way, there would be no time for further bad thoughts to enter my mind. If I had a bad thought after I'd asked for forgiveness, I'd go straight to hell, meet the devil with his pitchfork, and be doomed to beg for water forever.

Still, I was willing to take my chances. Even hell would be better than this.

But neither the devil nor Jesus showed up in my bedroom that day. I must have blacked out or fallen asleep, because the next thing I knew, I was on my bed with my mother beside me, holding me in her arms. Had she come home from work and found me in the closet? I didn't think about it then, but she must have been able to open the door even with the dresser pushed in front of it. Which means that my father could have gotten into the room if he'd really wanted to, or tried. Her voice trembled as she read verses from her Bible aloud, put her hand on my head, and prayed. We lay that way until I stopped shaking.

"Don't leave me," I cried. "Promise that you won't leave me." I held on to her for dear life.

"It's Vietnam," she whispered. "Vietnam." Her face was pale. "Your father loves you. You have to know that."

"Can't we go away from here?" I whispered. I always had a bag packed and stowed in the back of my closet—just in case. I needed to be ready. The Boxcar Children in my favorite book series had packed suitcases and run away from their grandfather, and if things got too bad, I planned to do the same.

My mother held me closer but didn't answer my question.

"Don't ever tell anyone about this," she whispered through her tears. "Your father is a good person. This isn't his fault."

"I think we need help," I whimpered. "I don't want to live like this."

She pressed her Bible tight against her chest and closed her eyes. "We have to pray harder," she said. "If we pray to Jesus and follow His word, He'll make everything okay."

Pray harder. That was my mother's answer for everything.

I didn't say a word. I just curled up like a baby and turned my back against her.

Suddenly I was furious. I'd asked—begged—for help and her only answer was to pray harder. I'd been praying as hard as I could all my life and nothing ever changed—for me or for her. The longer I thought about my mother's reaction, the more enraged I became.

Looking back, I think that the insight I had into the seriousness of our situation at such a young age was a double-edged sword. On the one hand I was acutely aware of the chaos all around me, and on the other I was far too young to understand that I was not responsible for creating this bedlam in my world.

Day Four

"Don't be surprised if my father doesn't talk much," I say to Steve, a friend and member of my writers' workshop who has offered to accompany my boyfriend, Gurpreet, and me on the four-hour drive to pick up my mother in Knoxville. "In fact, don't even expect him to stay for lunch. He'll probably just drop my mother off and hightail it back home as fast as he can."

Steve already knows a bit about my father because I'd tried to write about him once before and then quit midway. I'd thought then that it was time to move on and write about something else, but I hadn't succeeded.

My father had met Gurpreet when he accompanied me on my last visit home. But they'd barely spoken to each other. In fact, I'd barely spoken to my father then, or he to me. It takes a lot of energy to avoid each other the way we do. Now I'm worried about how he'll be with not only Gurpreet but also Steve along.

I'd told my mother a couple of months ago that Gurpreet had moved in with me, so no doubt my father knew, too. What I didn't tell her was that he'd already been living with me for several months. "Living in sin," my mother called our decision. No doubt my father would agree. I'm worried that our living arrangement will be the white elephant in the room, and I'm anxious to avoid exacerbating an already uncomfortable situation.

My parents drive into the gas station where my friends and I are already waiting, and I instinctively stand back, trying to gauge my father's mood as they get out of the car. I give my mother a perfunctory hug and watch as he shakes hands with Steve and Gurpreet. My father is watching me as well, and then we simultaneously reach out to hug each other. We both pull away before we've barely touched, and I feel my heart racing. *What is he thinking?*

I am shocked when my father agrees to stay for lunch. Usually my mother has to beg, but she wouldn't have done that today anyway, not in front of Gurpreet and Steve.

The five of us are crammed around a table for four in a little Chinese restaurant a short way down the road from the gas station. My father and Steve immediately strike up a conversation about the traffic in Atlanta. This shocks me because I see my father as someone who barely talks to his own family, much less complete strangers. Gurpreet and my mother chat. I mainly watch from the sidelines, interjecting a comment from time to time. I want to ask my father if he's still willing to move forward with our phone conversations, but I'm hesitant to bring it up. Am I afraid that he'll say no or that he'll point out to me the fact that I seem to be the one who's having a hard time getting started?

Gurpreet is leaving for Belgium the next day on a last-minute business trip. This means that my mother and I will be alone together for a whole week. That scares me, too. I have a hard time separating myself from her, just as I did when I was a little girl. I'm also concerned about what might come up about my father. Will we continue to avoid talking about him, or will she bring up subjects I don't want to discuss with her? How does she really feel about my talking to my dad? I am curious, but at the same time, I don't really want to deal with any of that.

I suspect that Gurpreet is secretly glad to be leaving because I've told him how stressful it is when my mother comes to visit me. Also, things haven't been that great between us for a while now. We've been eating dinner separately, working in different rooms, and he goes to bed hours before I do. He constantly complains that my dogs take up too much of my time, and that I should not let them come into my house. I wonder if he volunteered for this trip.

At the table, much to my amazement, my father is the life of the party. He is the one asking questions: Where in Europe is Gurpreet headed? How long will he be there? What will he be doing?

Gurpreet answers. I cut in.

"Have you been to Europe?" I ask my father. I have known him for thirty-one years, and I don't know where he's been other than Vietnam.

He shakes his head. "No. Never was in Europe," he says. His eyes are soft now. He smiles a little. "Only Vietnam and Australia. I went to Japan once, but I never made it out of the airport."

"You went to Australia?" I ask. "I didn't know that."

"Went for R&R. Right in the middle of 'Nam. Went to Australia and never even saw it," he says.

I'm confused. "What do you mean you didn't see it?"

"I found a pub as soon as I got off the plane," he says a bit sheepishly. "I spent the whole week in that pub. Drank 'til I was crazy. I must have slept in the hotel upstairs, but I don't remember going back there. Someone must have carried me. After a week I had to go back to Vietnam."

My mother's eyes bulge. She thinks alcohol is liquid evil. I wonder if she knew he used to drink.

"You used to drink?" I practically shriek. I have to hear this again just to believe it. I don't ever remember my father taking a single drink.

"Every chance I got. Most soldiers do. Hard to do it back in the States, though, because I was only twenty when I left 'Nam. Drinking age was twenty-one."

I'd never thought about this before. My father was drafted and went to war, put his life on the line to serve his country, came back, and couldn't even buy a beer.

I found out later that during the Vietnam era many states changed their laws to allow eighteen-year-olds to drink. And most military bases, even those in states with a minimum drinking age of twenty-one, would allow active military personnel to drink on the base at eighteen. But I didn't know all that then.

I am ashamed to admit that back then I didn't know anything about Vietnam. I had never asked my father a single question about it and never paid attention when it came up in history class. I even took a course on Vietnam in graduate school, thinking I would finally force

myself to learn something about the war whose aftershocks continued to shake my family. Yet all I remember is the My Lai massacre,
when a group of U.S. Army soldiers went on a mass killing spree,
murdering several hundred unarmed women, children, and elderly
Vietnamese in South Vietnam. Many of the victims were also raped,
mutilated, beaten, and tortured. After I saw actual pictures of the
aftermath, I tuned out and spent all my class time writing poetry just
to distract myself.

"Couldn't vote either," my father continues. "Had to be twenty-
one back then to do that, too."

He shifts in his seat, looks around the restaurant.

My father is talking. About the war. With me. It seems so perfectly
natural. Why hadn't this ever happened before?

He talks about the time when he went to the federal building in
Roanoke, Virginia, and appeared before a panel that finally agreed
to give him his full disability. Initially, he'd been declared 10 percent disabled, and over time he'd been reassessed as 20, then 30, and
finally 50 percent. Each time he'd appealed, and this time, he said, he
took a tape recorder with him in a big black bag.

"Bet they thought I'd brought a gun with me," he says. "I told them
fellers they weren't recording me unless I recorded them." My father
lets out a big, booming laugh. He sits back in his seat. "I left that day
with my disability."

I cannot get over the fact that my father is talking about the war so
matter-of-factly, and even with humor. Gurpreet and Steve are clearly
captivated and listening eagerly to his stories. And what's equally
surprising is that my mother appears to be taking it all in stride.

My father talks about feeling the mist when the planes overhead sprayed Agent Orange in the jungle and how the gunships came in and dropped weapons for the guys on the ground. He talks about a gunship named *Puff the Magic Dragon*. "'Send *Puff* out here,' we used to say when we called our superiors to tell them we needed more weapons. 'Send *Puff* out this way.'"

I hadn't known about this, but it suddenly explains my father's obsession with that Peter, Paul, and Mary song. He used to play and sing it all the time, and it always seemed to make him happy. I'd sing along, and it made me happy, too. In the song, Puff was a magic dragon who lived near the ocean in a place called Honah Lee. I wanted to live there, too; who wouldn't? But Honaker, Virginia, wasn't anything like the land of Honah Lee. We did go to the ocean once, but it didn't turn out to be anything like the magical escape I had dreamed about.

When I was nine, we went to Myrtle Beach. It was our first and only big trip away from home, the only family vacation we ever took.

My father went with my mother and me to the beach on the first day. A couple of hours were all he could endure. There were too many screaming children, too many shrieking seagulls. It was more noise than he could stand.

He helped me build a sandcastle, then waded out into the water to his knees. He stood there, gazing into the horizon as the water lapped around him.

"Look, Daddy! Look at me!" I yelled, half thrilled and half terrified. I was waist deep in the ocean already, my feet dug firmly into the sand so I wouldn't be knocked over by a wave.

He did not look.

"Come back," my mother, fully clothed, called from the shore. She did not believe Jesus would like it if she wore a swimsuit. "You've gone out too far," she yelled, her hand shading her eyes from the sun.

In her mind, the beach was a dangerous place. There were sharks. Jellyfish. Crabs that would snap your toes off in an instant. Malaria-ridden mosquitoes. The beach was a place where people went to have sex, to drink, to throw their glass bottles on the ground. Careful where you step. The glass will slice your feet.

The ocean was a foreign place, far away from my mother's mountains. It was to be respected, feared.

I loved the way the waves lapped against my body. They were warm. They tickled.

I looked back toward the shore. More people than I had ever seen at one time, in all colors, shapes, and sizes, lay stretched out as far as the eye could see. I felt safe there in the water, far away from them all, close to my father for once.

"Delmer, get her!" my mother hollered. "She's gone too far. She's going to drown!"

Her voice sounded far away.

I planted myself in the sand, dug my feet in past my ankles. If I could dig down far enough, ground myself in this place, I wouldn't be pulled out to sea.

My father didn't budge; he just continued to watch the horizon.

Hands waving frantically, my mother removed her shoes and waded ankle-deep into the surf.

"Come back," she called. "Both of you, come back."

But today we're sitting together in a restaurant on the road to Atlanta, and my father is finally talking.

"How did you find out you had to go to the war?" I ask. "Did you get a letter in the mail?"

"I got the letter when I was eighteen—almost nineteen," he says. "That was in nineteen sixty-seven. When they did my physical, they told me I was flatfooted and color-blind, said I had been that way my whole life. I didn't know, but it didn't seem to bother them. 'We got you, boy,' they told me. 'Don't play dumb. You ain't goin' nowhere.' I guess they was gonna send me over there no matter what was wrong with me."

My mother's hands are folded in front of her face now. She looks like she might cry. I hold my breath and pray she won't. I can't stand to see my mother cry. My whole life, I have seen too much of that.

"By the time I got to Vietnam, it was April of nineteen sixty-nine," my father says. "It was after the Tet Offensive, the worst time to be drafted."

"What is the Tet Offensive?" I ask. It's embarrassing to be so ignorant, but I really have no idea. It's just one of the many things about the war I've managed not to know. Tet must certainly have been discussed in my college course, but I've totally blocked it out.

"A bunch of North Vietnamese broke into the citadel in Hue, took it over. This was on Tet, the Vietnamese New Year. Nobody ever thought that would happen. They flew the Communist flag. America saw right then and there this wasn't going to be a fast war. The American people went berserk, turned against their own. They stopped supporting the war, hated us soldiers like devils. They'd thought

America would swoop in, quickly help the South win the war, and then get right back out. But it didn't happen. We soldiers, though, we weren't doing anything wrong. We were just following orders."

I don't know what to say. I am so surprised to be hearing my father talk this way that I am at a loss for words. I had never once considered the fact that my father would be able to tell me about the war in its historical context. I am appalled to hear that the American people turned against their own soldiers. Today the last people we'd ever blame are the troops themselves.

I am hobbled (and humbled) by my ignorance; Steve asks my father if he had symptoms of Agent Orange, if he knew what it was back then.

"I just knew it killed the plants," my father says. "They came down in planes and sprayed it all over everything like crop dusters. I didn't even know until ten years later that the stuff was called Agent Orange or what harm it could do. That big mass didn't come on my lungs until a few years after that."

He'd had part of one lobe of his right lung removed when I was in college. He'd also had several surgeries to remove cysts from his fingers, which luckily didn't seem to have any effect on his ability to play the guitar. The doctors had said both conditions might have been caused by Agent Orange.

"Once it's in your body, it stays with you," my mother had explained to me when he was having one of his surgeries. "It never leaves."

Like the war, I added silently.

My father grins. "Dumbness comes from Agent Orange, too. That's one reason I'm like this."

Then, suddenly, his eyes appear tired. He looks wrinkled and old, his skin loose around the sides of his cheeks. He is the spitting image of his mother. I'd never noticed that before. It's been a long time since I really looked at him up close, and it upsets me to see how much he's aged while I've been trying to distance myself from him.

"All those doctors wanted to dope me up, put me on all kinds of drugs, but I told those suckers—told them that my guitar does more for me than any drug I've ever had."

I remember all those birthdays, all those Christmases, when my father locked himself away in his room, playing his guitar instead of being with us. At night, I fell asleep to the sound of that guitar. In the morning, I awoke to it. It was his lifeline. Still is.

As a child, I loved to hear him play, but a part of me was also jealous of that guitar. No matter how sick he was, no matter how long he locked himself in his room, he always had his guitar with him. It was the first thing he reached for, the one thing in the world that always made him happy.

"Who is the best guitar player in the world?" he used to ask me, midsong, as I sat at his feet.

"You are," I'd always yell, knowing it would make him smile.

My father shakes his head and looks down at his hands. "I did some things that were wrong, but I always tell people that I made it out the other side. I made it," he says. "I survived. I was in Vietnam for twelve months, and then I got out of that place."

Everyone is silent. I take a deep breath and nod.

My father's food is still untouched on his plate.

• • •

"I can't believe he talked. I can't believe he was social," I say to my mother on the drive home.

Finally it seems to me that he just might talk to me when I call to interview him after all.

"He's been that way for about five years now," my mother says quietly from the backseat.

Both Steve and Gurpreet had tried to get her to sit up front, but she'd refused. So Steve sits in the front seat next to me, and Gurpreet is in back with my mom.

"He's friendlier now," she goes on. "He's okay with strangers. He's often in a good mood these days. Your father has changed." Her words, stated so matter-of-factly, hit me like a blow to the chest. How could I not have known? Why hadn't I known this was happening? But, of course, I hadn't wanted to know. My whole adult life had been spent trying not to know what was going on with my father.

I am suddenly embarrassed, wondering what Gurpreet and Steve must think of me as a daughter.

"I think it's because of those CDs," my mother continues. "Ever since he started traveling around and singing in all those churches. Since he took the songs he wrote and put them on a CD. He wrote a song about Vietnam. Did you know that?"

I did, vaguely, but I don't remember it. I don't know the words. I knew he'd recorded a couple of CDs that were played on WGTH radio, and that, as a result, he'd started receiving calls asking him to play at various churches, weddings, and even funerals in the area.

He'd been doing that for at least the past five years, and he'd given me the CDs a few years ago for Christmas. But I'd never played them. It actually made me angry to think that he had become such a celebrity in the community after all the time my mother and I had spent, and all we'd gone through, trying to protect him from public scrutiny. Now, all of a sudden, he was out and about, actually socializing. I didn't want to believe it was possible. I didn't want to acknowledge that there could be anything good about my father. So I just stuck those CDs behind the glass doors of the TV stand and refused to listen to them. Eventually, I forgot I even had them.

"Besides the song he wrote, though, this was the first time you'd ever heard Dad talk about the war, right?" I ask my mother on the drive back to Atlanta. I am sure she didn't know any of this either.

I see her shake her head in the rearview mirror. "He told me most of it a while ago," she says. "I'd heard most of it before."

My face drops. I didn't know that either. She was the person who told me I could *never* ask him about Vietnam, and now I find out they actually have talked about it. I feel instantly jealous and somehow betrayed.

I don't say anything, but for the rest of the drive I'm silently stewing, and becoming increasingly disturbed about all the things I now realize I haven't known about my father, while my mother talks cheerily with Gurpreet and Steve.

• • •

We're back in Atlanta, and my mother and Gurpreet have already gone inside when Steve tells me he's confused.

"Confused about what?" I ask as I zip my windbreaker against the November chill. It's been colder than usual for November in Georgia.

"Your dad," he says. "You'd never know anything was wrong with him. Are you sure he has PTSD? Don't you think you're exaggerating?"

I'm furious but don't want Steve to see.

"I'm not exaggerating," I say coldly. I can't believe we're having this conversation. Steve and I have been in the same writers' group ever since I moved to Atlanta. He knows I've been trying to write about my father for years. "You weren't there when I was a kid. You don't know the way things were."

"Christal, your father laughed and talked about the war," Steve says. "He wasn't creepy or angry. He *wanted* to talk to you. It's hard to believe that the two of you never talked much. It doesn't make sense."

"What about it don't you understand?" I growl impatiently. I am less concerned with Steve seeing my anger now.

"I don't think your father has PTSD," he says. "I wonder if you made it up. You were pretty messed up back then. You've said it yourself."

I have always admired Steve for speaking his mind, but this time he's gone too far. I want to punch him in the face, to scream at him to get away from me and never come back.

This is what I have always been most afraid of: finally telling the truth and people not believing it.

I tell Steve I might see him at our writers' group meeting next month, although I know I won't be attending. I barely say good-bye as he walks off. His words have cut me so deeply that I don't want to see his face anymore. How dare he imply that all the horrible things I went through as a child were figments of my imagination?

Journal

In my hometown people did not ask questions. You were expected to accept what was because it had always been. You followed the rules; you did not veer from the norms.

People saw things as black or white, good or bad. There was no in between, no room for gray. God was ever present and very tangible, as was the devil, and each thought or action put you one step closer to heaven or hell.

Psalm 78 says that God "rained down manna upon them [the Israelites] to eat, and had given them of the corn of heaven," so I knew that in heaven, you'd eat corn and walk down streets of gold. Everyone would live in a mansion. In hell, you'd thirst for all eternity, beg for a single drop of water forever. There was fire in hell, fire made to burn you.

Drinking alcohol, having sex before marriage, cursing, using drugs, and watching R-rated movies were sins. Partake in any of these (or a million other things that would offend God), and you were on the road to hell.

Christianity was the beacon of light, Jesus Christ the son who would wash your sins away.

You didn't tell people about your problems. You brought your problems before the Lord.

You and the Lord were expected to have a personal relationship. It was He with whom you'd share all your secrets. He would make things better if you trusted in Him enough, if you followed the Bible exactly.

At first, I tried to talk to Him about the war, about the gun my father took to the river, the pads he slept on to absorb his night sweats, the wild and crazy look that would come into his eyes when he was startled.

My father had lost his temper and snapped on many occasions. I loved him, yet I feared him. I longed for him to touch me, to hold me, yet I was terrified of his mood swings, his tendency to snap at the least little thing, to shake and writhe in anger at the drop of a dime. I avoided him as best as I could. We both spent a lot of time locked away—him in his bedroom and me in my closet.

Sometimes, when he was curled up in bed like a baby I'd crack open the door to peek in. *He must hate me something awful,* I thought. *He must hate my mother, too.* His face was always to the wall, as if he couldn't even stand to look our way. Sometimes I'd sit in his room and look at the pictures of him in his soldier's uniform. He looked so sad and serious. His war medals hung in a perfectly straight row in a glass-enclosed display case I was *never* to touch.

"Make it all stop," I begged the Lord. "I'll do anything if you'll make him love us."

When nothing changed after a few months, I looked to myself. I must be doing something wrong. Maybe I wasn't good enough to earn the privilege of happiness. I was clearly being punished because I was a horrible person.

My mother and I protected him, walked on eggshells, and did anything and everything not to provoke him. We knew no other way. I spent my childhood wondering if he was a bad person, a lousy father, or if the war really had made him what he was.

"It's not his fault," my mother said. "Not his fault. Not his fault," as if she could convince herself the more she said it. "It's Vietnam," she always added, lowering her voice as if the word itself were unspeakable. We spent our lives hiding from that war, though it raged all around us.

Day Five

I t's 10:30 the night after my mother arrived. I'm in my office, working on the computer, when her cell phone rings. It is my father.

She starts out talking in a normal tone of voice, moves to a whisper, then goes into my bedroom and closes the door. She's accustomed to hiding; it's all she knows.

Ten minutes later, she comes into my office. Her face is red and swollen. She is crying, phone in hand.

My heart beats faster. It's hard to breathe. I have seen this look before.

My father has had an "episode." I know it. I don't have to ask.

My father is angry. He has turned, snapped, short-circuited.

I know without asking that it's because of the things we talked about the day before. When he was talking about drinking he'd suddenly looked up and asked me if I'd ever done drugs. I was surprised by the question, and before I even thought about it I said that I'd tried pot a long time ago. Bad idea. He looked startled and said that he'd never once used drugs. When he was in Vietnam everyone else was smoking pot every night, and he was proud of the fact that he'd never done that. Now he has this wild notion I am hooked on drugs, slowly killing myself, my mother tells me.

"I tried to tell him. I tried to tell him," she whispers. "He's not making sense. This doesn't make sense."

She repeats this over and over as if saying it often enough would make it make sense.

"You have to talk to him," she pleads.

She tells me she hung up on him. When he gets like this, it is impossible to talk to him, but she's desperate and afraid he's going to hurt himself. I have to take care of my mother now, pick up the broken pieces, take care of us both, the way I always have. I don't know if I can do that anymore.

She dials his number and sticks the phone to my ear. "Talk to him. Please," she says. "Maybe he'll talk to you."

I brace myself, take a deep breath. I sit down on the bed. Why am I always the one who has to fix things? Isn't that what parents are supposed to do for their children? Now it feels as if I have to be the parent, and I'm terrified that I'll fail. For once I just want to be the child.

It is absolutely outlandish that my father thinks I'm using drugs. This is crazy. Absolutely crazy. He's gone berserk. I don't even take Tylenol if I have a headache. But he wouldn't know that.

"Hello," he says, answering the phone after the third ring. His voice sounds surprisingly calm, but I don't trust him. I expect him to scream in my ear, to shout, to blame me for I don't know what. To tell me that he cannot talk about the war with me; it will bring up too many memories he won't be able to handle. It will send him over the edge.

"Dad?" I say, already cringing because I don't know what will come. I remember this feeling from when I was a child.

"I'm not using drugs, Dad," I say. "I swear I'm not using drugs. I teach school. I wouldn't do that. I promise, okay?"

I want to get off the phone and tell him that I cannot reason with a crazy person.

I don't.

Instead I tell him that I love him, that it meant a lot to hear him talk about the war at the restaurant, and that everything is going to be okay. I say it over and over. I don't know if I believe it.

"I love you, Dad. I love you," I say. "I'm not using drugs."

When he speaks, his voice is gentle. There is no trace of anger. No violence. No hate.

"I believe you," he says.

He has come back to his senses again. Just like that.

"Your guitar and your music are your drugs, Dad, like my animals are mine," I say. I'm crying now, tears rolling down my face. I don't make a sound, don't want him to know. It would hurt him if he knew he'd hurt me, and I don't want to hurt him. My feelings are swinging wildly from anger to despair, just the way his have always done.

"I have a story to tell just like you do, and I need your help. You're part of my story, and I just want to get to know you. For you to get to know me. It's been thirty-one years," I say.

There is a thick silence between us.

"Okay," he finally says, his voice shaky. "I'll help you."

He is still unsure about this.

"We can talk about whatever you want," I say. "No pressure."

Another long pause.

"You can ask me some questions sometime," he says timidly.

I take a deep breath. He's willing to move forward—at least for now—with letting me try to get to know him. Perhaps this day will end on a good note after all.

"Thank you, Dad," I say with true sincerity as we hang up the phone.

• • •

My mother and I lie awake all night in my bed staring at the ceiling. She has Parkinson's disease, although it's hard to tell during the day when her medication is in full swing. At night, when the medicine wears off, she can hardly move. She's trapped inside her own body and can't even speak clearly. She struggles to sit up in bed so she can breathe. Nights are the worst.

My mother has always been the person I've thought of as my "family." I have no brothers and sisters, and I'd spent my whole life trying to separate from my father. I'd always wondered what would happen if she weren't in the picture anymore. Would I ever go back home at all? Until recently, I'd have said that I wouldn't. I'd have closed the door on my father and tried to move on the best I could. Now I don't know what I'd do. He's finally opening up to me, and I'm no longer so certain that walking away from him would be my best option.

My mother turns toward me. "Why do you think we never told anyone?" she asks, her words slurred.

Why is she asking this now? The question hangs in the air between us as I struggle to find an answer.

So many thoughts flood my mind. *We didn't tell because no one would have believed us. We didn't tell because we were afraid. We didn't tell because we worried we'd be ostracized by our community. We didn't tell because my father might have been taken away. We didn't tell because it was easier to try to pretend none of it had happened.*

I don't know if any or all of these are the right answer. The only thing I know for sure—and what I say—is, "We didn't tell because we didn't know how, Mom."

She nods and stares at the ceiling again, her eyes filled with tears. And again the room is silent.

Journal

When I was growing up, I hated going out to eat with my father.

It never failed. Someone always dropped a plate or a spoon and sent him into a frenzy, his eyes wild and crazy. He'd let out a yell, leap a foot in the air, and right there in the restaurant, be ready to fight. Afterward, his hands would shake so badly he could barely eat his food. My mother and I knew not to speak to him then, but I knew that everyone else in the restaurant was staring at him and whispering about us. Every time that happened I just wanted to curl up in a little ball and become invisible.

After one of those episodes, he'd drive like a madman on the way home. Traffic lights and stop signs were only suggestions.

"So stupid," he'd say to my mother and me under his breath, mashing his foot down hard on the gas pedal. "You're both so stupid. You ain't got the sense God gave a goose."

This was the one thing he said to us more than anything else, as if we were somehow at fault for what happened.

And every time my mother just sat in the front seat next to him and cried. She didn't try to stop him from saying cruel things or ask him to slow down because she knew it wouldn't do any good.

Other times, however, he could be very calm, especially when he went to church to play his guitar and sing. Or when we'd all go to his music buddies' houses, where I'd sit sleepy-eyed until late at night while they played "Just as I Am" and "Amazing Grace." I'd drift off to sleep on a sofa while he played and my mother sat beside me, smiling and clapping her hands. He wasn't ever mean to us when there was music.

But as his mood swings became more and more frequent I became more and more terrified of his unpredictability, to the point where, by the time I was eleven, I couldn't even acknowledge that there was another side to his personality.

One time, I used a cassette recorder to capture my father's rantings and played them back so that he could hear what a horrible person he was.

"This is who you are," I yelled. "You are a horrible person, and I hate you! You are stupid! So stupid."

I taunted him for wearing hats and belt buckles that signified he was a veteran, told him he was an embarrassment to society.

A look of sadness came over his face when I said that, but he never responded. Not when I mentioned the war.

Day Six

I call my father before 6:00 the next morning to check on him. I've been up all night thinking about him, but he sounds better than I expect and wants to know how my mother and I slept. I do not lie. I tell him I was up all night. I was worried about him. I'm relieved he's okay—*glad* he's okay.

"You shouldn't stay up on my account," he says by way of apology. He sounds more energetic, happier than the night before.

I don't want him to forget our agreement. Things change fast for him. I need to remind him often. I'll need to be reminded that he's okay. But for now at least, things seem to be going well.

Once more, I tell him that I love him, and I thank him for agreeing to talk to me and answer some questions.

"You're welcome," he says. His voice is steady.

"I'll call you again tomorrow," I tell him, hoping that this mood will last.

I hand my mother the phone. Her voice is normal. She doesn't try to hide or whisper. She chats for a while and tells him about our plans for today. We're going to the zoo, then cleaning my house from top to bottom. She frowns at the end of the call, tells him she loves him, and then puts the phone on the bed.

I can tell by her expression that he's said something she doesn't like. I wish she wouldn't tell me, but I know that she will. I'm the only person who knows the truth about us. About him. It's too much to carry alone.

"He says he hopes you don't ruin him," my mother says.

His words gouge a hole through my heart. I know exactly what he means, and my mother knows it, too. He worries that if I write about our conversations, and if the people in my parents' community find out about his PTSD, they won't ask him to come sing and play his guitar anymore. He worries he'll be judged, and that he'll be ostracized.

It's something that's weighed heavily on my mind, too. I know it's time to acknowledge the truth about what happened to my family because of Vietnam, and I feel compelled to write about the process, but what cost will it have for us all? I struggle to reconcile what I know is the right thing with what I fear the people in Honaker will think and say about us.

I wish Gurpreet were here to hold me and tell me stories about India to take my mind off my problems.

Journal

On our trip to Myrtle Beach when I was nine, my father refused to come out of the motel room after the first day. My mother and I stayed by the pool from that point on. We could see the door of our room from there.

"Put your sunscreen on," my mother told me, her eyes never leaving the door.

I didn't rub the sunscreen on my body. It was too much trouble. I stuck my tongue out at her, held my nose, and jumped off the diving board. It went on all day long like that, my mother reminding me to lather myself with sunscreen and my not doing what I was told. She wasn't watching anyway.

That night, back in the motel room, while we ate potted meat on crackers and slurped cheddar cheese soup from our thermoses, my skin was on fire and I was shivering.

When my father noticed that I was shaking with chills from my sunburn, he screamed at my mother. "What were you thinking! What were you thinking what were you thinking what were you thinking!" He huffed and puffed like he was going to blow the room apart, got so red that I half expected him to explode, a million pieces of himself strewn all over the room.

I was in bed, under the covers, trying to stay warm as I ate. I pulled the blanket over my head and, through a peephole in the side, watched my mother cowering on the pullout sofa they slept on. She didn't say a word. My father had never actually hit her, but I knew the verbal abuse cut her to the core.

I wanted to tell him that I was okay, that it wasn't her fault, but I was as afraid as she was to speak.

After about twenty minutes he calmed down, as if a switch in his brain had flipped off. He crawled onto the pullout sofa beside my mother, propped himself up with a couple of pillows, and turned on the TV as if nothing had happened.

"It's probably a good thing I never had any more kids," my mother said to me the next morning when we were once again alone at the pool. "I wouldn't want anyone else to go through what we go through," she continued, positioning me so she could simultaneously lather me with sunscreen and keep an eye on the motel door behind me. She looked at me and tried to smile. "Would you want that, Christal?"

She needed validation that I was okay with being the only person to share her secret. I did not flinch. "No," I said.

Sometimes it was the truth. There were times I'd never wish the life we had on anyone else. But other times—most other times, in fact—I longed for a sibling so much I ached inside. The more people who shared our secret, the less each of us would hurt. This *was* the case, wasn't it?

Looking back, I see that my mother needed a confidant as much as I did. And it makes me sad that the only one she had to confide in was me. But it also makes me angry that she thought it was okay to talk about such things with a nine-year-old kid. Why did I always have to share her burdens as well as carrying my own, not to mention my father's? It was too much.

Day Seven

"Why do you want to know about the war so much?" my therapist asks when I see her this afternoon.

This question has many answers.

"I want to know more about my father," I tell her truthfully. "The war is a big part of him."

"There are many ways to get to know a person," she says. "And many ways to forgive him."

My therapist is a mind reader. Her words make me nervous. I hadn't planned on talking about forgiveness. Haven't I already done that? Suddenly, I'm not sure. How does a person know for sure that she's forgiven someone? I do not know the answer to that question.

Of course you have forgiven him, I tell myself. *You wouldn't even be talking to him if you hadn't forgiven him.*

Of course I have forgiven him. Haven't I?

I won't press my father tonight. I'll let him lead. I'm worried that if I ask him about the war he'll put a bullet through his head and no one will be there to stop him. I decide that I won't mention the war unless he does.

When I call, I talk about my dogs Arthur and Duma. The weather. How my mother and I spent the day.

"Some veterans exaggerate," my father says out of the blue. "I don't go to group meetings anymore." He *wants* to talk about the war. He is ready.

By "group meetings," he means group *therapy*, but he will not say it. I remember when he went to those meetings. I was a teenager. He didn't go for long.

"Everyone tried to outdo each other with all their stories," he says. "The first feller would tell a story about what he did, then the next one would make sure his story was worse. I couldn't stand it."

Without my asking him anything he starts to tell me about being a radio carrier. He carried a radio in a backpack for his squad leader. Eight or nine people were in his squad. He says he was in the Americal Division, First Battalion, Sixth Infantry.

I don't know what any of this means, but I make a mental note to look it up later.

The radio weighed twenty pounds, and he had to change frequencies often so the enemy wouldn't hear. If he screwed up, everyone in his squad would die.

"Ask him if anyone in his family ever wrote him when he was over there," my mother whispers. She sits beside me and tries to listen in.

My father is the youngest of ten brothers and sisters. No one went to Vietnam but him. My mother has told me before that he got little family support.

I ask the question.

"My mom wrote," he says. "One sister and brother-in-law did. That's all."

This shocks me and it doesn't shock me. My father has always been distant with his family, and they with him. Was it this way when he was a child, too?

Years ago, my mother made it her life mission to get my father's mother to tell us that she loved us.

"Tell Mamaw Presley that you love her. Don't forget," she'd stage whisper, nudging me with her elbow.

It took Mamaw ten years to say it back to me. I don't remember her ever saying it to my father.

"No one in my family knew much about the war," my father continues. "We didn't have a TV. They never listened to the radio much. Mom never said anything in her letters about the demonstrations or the protests. I didn't know what was going on here in the States. After the war was over, when I was flying back to Fort Hood in Texas, one boy on the plane told me, 'You better change into civilian clothes first thing you do, because they will spit all over you.'

"I didn't know what he was talking about," my father says, "but sure enough, that boy was right. Soon as I walked out of the airport, people were lined up in the hundreds, holding signs that read 'Baby Killers,' spitting all over the boys still in their uniforms. I put my head down and walked past them as fast as I could."

His voice is shaky now, and I feel my body tensing up. I don't know which way this is going to go. It could be the start of one of his episodes. He could fly into a rage or shut down completely. Or he could pull himself together.

I want to change the subject, ask him about something else. Anything else. He does not give me that chance. He speaks quickly, pushes the words from his throat like bullets.

"I don't look at things on Vietnam anymore, like those books you got me last year for Christmas. When you come home, you can have those if you want," he says. "I don't mind having them, but I don't want to look at them. I don't want to bring back bad memories."

Hearing him say that, I feel awful. I'd bought my father two encyclopedias of the Vietnam War, complete with color pictures on almost every page. My reasoning at the time was that the only things I'd ever seen him read when I was a child were books or magazines about Vietnam. It had always seemed strange to me that he could be so disturbed by the war and still read anything he could get his hands on about it. But that's the way it was, and I just assumed that nothing had changed.

"I hate that I done the things I done," he says, his voice urgent but steady. "I know I did some things I shouldn't have done. I knew better. I did. I . . . I just didn't consider those people human. I never saw a Vietnamese before in my life, and I hated them. We didn't even call them Vietnamese back then. Called them Charlies, dinks, and gooks. That's all I knew. They taught us that. I was trained not to see them as human. The government can say whatever they want, but they trained us that way. It hurt me more to see a dog or cat dead than them Vietnamese. The government likes young boys who ain't got no sense. Easier to train, easier to brainwash that way."

As soon as he pauses I jump in before he can continue. I've heard enough for today, and I'm afraid that if he continues much longer he really will fly off the handle and I'll be the one responsible.

"I love you, Dad," I tell him. "There's someone on the other line, and I have to go now." And I quickly hang up, before he can even respond.

Then I immediately feel guilty, as if I'd abandoned him. But my hands are trembling. I don't know if I can keep going with these conversations. I worry they're going to push one—or both—of us over the edge. But, at the same time, I'm even more afraid that if I let go of him now, I'll lose him forever.

Journal

The trailer we lived in was falling apart, but nothing much could be done about it. I used to pray that we wouldn't get any bad storms because the wind would blow the siding off.

My father had the idea of putting truck tires on the roof to anchor it down like all our neighbors did. My mother cried when he said it because, she said, we had the nicest trailer in New Garden Estates and the tires were going to ruin the looks of it.

He told her we'd still have the nicest trailer—even with the tires on the roof. Besides that, maybe next year we'd get a new roof, or maybe even a house someday. He didn't smile much, but he smiled then.

He made everything okay.

He never did put those tires on our roof. Instead, he came home the next day with metal clamps and spent the whole evening and into the night on top of the trailer, securing our roof.

It was later that year, when Desert Storm came, that he got much worse and finally got his disability and stopped working. It seemed weird to me that when a war came up that he didn't even fight in, he went bonkers like I have never seen. He couldn't take being around noise or around other people. He sat home for months and locked himself in his room. He stopped playing music and going to church, and he stopped showering or changing clothes. I could hardly stand to go into my parents' bedroom because it smelled so bad, but every time I did he was always in the same spot, his eyes big and red, glued to the war on TV.

He went to the river a lot during Desert Storm, but he always came back. My mother cried a lot and read the Bible for comfort.

Alone in my bed at night I'd close my eyes and imagine her tucked beside me. In my mind, we held each other in the darkness and watched my black goldfish glide slowly through its tank, illuminated by the nightlight.

She'd stroke my hair and lay her head on my shoulder. "It'd be nice to be a fish," she'd say.

Day Eight

This evening, I go online and look up everything I can find on the Americal Division, First Battalion, Sixth Infantry. They were called "The Gunfighters." I find my father's name, Delmer Presley, listed on their website. I don't know why, but that sort of shocks me. Somehow it makes Vietnam not just something in his head but totally real.

There are hundreds of stories, hundreds of photographs there, but I don't look at them. Not yet. I'm not ready for that today.

Some of these men must have known my father. When I call him later I tell him about the website and ask him if he wants to contact any of these soldiers. Some of their addresses are listed. They have a reunion once a year.

"No," he says, so quickly it's clear that he doesn't even have to think about it.

"Why, Dad?" I hope I'm not pushing too much, but I want to know.

He sighs, lowers his voice. He sounds exhausted. "Maybe. Maybe one day. Wait and see."

I need to change the subject. He sounds so drained that I don't want to ask him any questions about the war today. I don't want to do anything to tire him any more than he already is.

"What are you doing right now?" I ask.

He is holding his cat named Avery, brushing its hair.

"Avery likes to hear me play the guitar," my father says. His voice is so low I can barely hear.

"What's wrong, Dad?" There is a lump in my throat now.

"I'm always depressed," he says.

I chew the sides of my nails so I won't bite them off like I usually do. "What can I do?" I ask.

"Bring a gun and shoot me." He laughs a little, a pretend laugh that he hopes I'll think is real.

I don't know what to say when he gets like this. I want to run, get as far away as I can, shut myself in a closet, and pull a blanket over my head. I am a little girl again.

I don't know how to help him. I am six hours away, and I don't know how to help him.

"You know I love you, right?" I say. I can think of nothing else.

"I love you, too," he says.

I have to think of something uplifting to talk about. I cannot let him linger in that place of darkness.

"Will we have Christmas in the cabin this year?" I ask. Over the past two years, my father has been building a cabin in the backyard from nothing but a pile of mismatched logs. He is working on the chimney now, building it from stones. As soon as the chimney is done, the cabin will be finished.

"There's no room in that cabin," he says.

"We can make room, move some things out."

"There are no lights," he says.

"Let's use candles."

"You'll burn the place down," he says.

There is a long silence between us.

"I'm the best dad in the world," he says, trying to muster up a laugh to cover the sarcasm.

"I'm the best child in the world," I say.

He laughs. A real laugh. Not pretend.

"Who told you that?" he asks.

"I don't need anyone to tell me," I say. I make sure my voice is strong. Steady. I am good at being strong, as good as he is at pretending.

"I wrote a poem for you," I tell him. Then, as soon as I say it, my stomach gets a kink. I don't know how he'll react. What if it upsets him more? I wish I'd just kept my mouth shut.

"Let's hear it," he says.

I start to tear up. "Maybe I'll read it tomorrow. I'll cry if I read it today."

Another silence.

"Do you want me to read it?" I ask, hesitantly.

"Do you want to read it?"

"I guess I can read it today," I say, although I'm not entirely sure I'll get through it.

I think about a beach when I read it. Palm trees. I am lying in the sun. Far away from here. I won't cry if I remove myself from the situation. I am a master at this; I've done it thousands of times before.

There is a voice in the background now, a little girl reading a poem to her father. She is not me.

Daddy, I know why you went to the river
With that gun.
I know.
You did not want us to find
Your body.
You loved us too much for that,
Tried to save us from the mess.
I did not understand.
Not back then.
Instead, I ran from your war,
Avoided your foxhole,
Went to sleep while you kept watch,
Stayed away as long as I could.
And longer.
But I'm here now.
I'm here.
This time to stay.
This time to fight the war beside you,
To go into the river with you,
To keep watch this time so
You can fall asleep.
If only you'll let me.

My heart is beating a mile a minute by the time I finish. But inside I feel relieved, as if a mass within has been purged.

"That's good," he says. "I don't understand it, though. I'm not smart enough to figure it out."

"Stop it, Dad."

He is kidding around now.

"What do you really think?" I ask. I need his approval now.

"I'm going to put you back in my will," he says.

That is funny. His jokes are good—occasionally.

"Dad, do you remember anything that happened back then?" I ask. I have to know.

"No, I don't," he says. "Don't remember much of anything. Why—do you?"

"I remember some things," I say. I feel small, like a child again.

"Christal, if something happens to me, don't you let my guitars go for nothing. Don't sell those guitars for nothing. They're worth a lot of money. I've got some silver dollars, too, and those are worth something. Don't you let that stuff go for peanuts." He is talking fast again, getting louder all the while.

"Don't talk like that, Dad. You're going to live a long time. You have a long life ahead of you. You're still young."

"Don't you let that stuff go for nothing," he says. "Promise me you won't."

I promise.

Journal

My father rarely opened Christmas presents with my mother and me. I could always hear him playing the guitar in the next room as I yanked the wrapping paper off each gift and moved on to the next, and to the next.

"This one is from your father. He really loves you," my mother would say at perfectly regular intervals, while the sound of "Amazing Grace" drifted down the hallway. "He might not know how to show it, but he does," she'd add for good measure.

Somehow he always knew when I had finished. Suddenly the strumming would stop, and a few seconds later the door would ease open. I'd bolt down the hall then like a mad person yelling, "I'm here, Dad! I'm here," in case he'd forgotten. But he never did, no matter how much I worried he would. He always emerged with a tired smile, his guitar hung on his shoulder, with a special present for me.

It was always grand, the thing I had wanted the most, and the card was always cheap, with glitter that flaked off on my hands.

LOVE, DADDY, he always signed in capital letters, though I never called him that. At the bottom was always a lopsided heart he had drawn himself. Our fingers were so close as he handed me that card.

It was the same year after year. Only the wrinkles in his face and the color of his hair changed.

Late that night, stuffed to the point of explosion on popcorn and chocolate, I would sit at my father's feet and sing "Just as I Am," and "The Old Rugged Cross," while his magic fingers plucked the strings. My mother waved her hands all the while and walked back and forth, warning us we were being so loud the whole town could hear.

"That is the point!" my father would yell, in his deep, booming voice. He looked old and worn even when he laughed.

"Who is the best guitar player in the world?" he hollered.

"You are!" I'd yell back.

When it came to music, no sound was too loud for this man who hated loud noises.

Day Nine

On Thanksgiving Day my mother gets it in her mind that she has to leave the next day. She was supposed to stay two more days, but she has to get back there to take care of my father the way she always does.

She calls home twice. He doesn't pick up. She calls her mother to ask if he's been there. Did he go there for Thanksgiving dinner? What was he like? What time did he leave?

It takes thirty minutes to get to their house from my grandmother's. It's already been an hour since he left. He should have been there by now, she tells me.

She doesn't realize that keeping track of him and worrying like this is not normal. Her lack of awareness frustrates me, but I know there's nothing I can do to change it.

When he does finally call her back, he says tomorrow won't work. He's playing his guitar at a funeral and has some other things to do.

He can't meet us at the halfway point. She'll have to stick with the original plan.

I am relieved. He is going out, doing things, keeping himself busy. He's not giving his guitars away, not getting rid of those silver dollars. I have seen him far worse than this, but my mother is upset. She thinks she needs to be there.

At my suggestion, my mother and I had our Thanksgiving dinner at a local Indian restaurant. Neither one of us had the energy to cook. Mom hates Indian food, but during the months Gurpreet and I have been living together we've cooked Indian food almost every night. Foolishly, I'd hoped that eating the familiar food would lessen the pain of his absence. Or maybe I just wanted to punish her for no reason, and I knew that she would never have the gumption to object.

Now I need to take a walk, calm the voices in my head, put some distance between my mother and me. I know she won't like it and that she'll want to go with me, but I won't let her.

I wonder sometimes if she understands my father at all.

Right now he needs his space, needs to clear his head, needs our support from a distance. When I come back from my walk, I will lock myself in my room and stay a while. We have a lot in common, my father and me.

• • •

"You should go to the library to get some books on Vietnam," my father says when I call him later that evening. He says he is going to make sure I learn some things about the war in this process.

"I can't go today," I tell him, assuming that's what he meant. "It's Thanksgiving, and anyway it's too late. I'll go tomorrow, Dad."

"What's Mom doing now?" he wants to know.

He *would* have to mention her. I'm annoyed with her right now, and she's the last thing I want to talk about.

"I don't know," I say bluntly.

"What do you mean you don't know?"

"I don't know where she is. She's somewhere in the house. We're not getting along right now. I've locked myself in my office."

"What happened?" He is clearly concerned.

"I got mad at her," I admit reluctantly. "I told her she needed to leave you alone, stop fretting so much. I like to be alone when I'm angry. I don't like it when people come around. It smothers me." I have never talked to him like this before. I am surprised how easy it is once I get started. I hope my openness doesn't make him shut down.

"I'm like that, too," he says. "I want to be alone. I like it better that way."

"I guess we're a lot alike then, Dad." The words are surprisingly easy to say. I am the spitting image of my father in more ways than one, and it's not as painful as I thought it would be to acknowledge that.

"Do you get along good with yourself, Christal? Do you like yourself?"

I hesitate before I answer. Of course I like myself. *Don't I?*

"Of course I like myself," I say doubtfully.

He does not respond.

"I like myself most days," I clarify. "Some days I like myself so much that I'd rather be alone than with other people."

"You sound like an old maid," he says. I cannot tell if he's being funny or if he's really worried about me now.

"I'm not an old maid, Dad. I'm social when I want to be, when I'm in the mood."

"You're like me," he says. He sounds happy about that.

"We like ourselves better than anybody we've ever run into."

He has misunderstood me. "I don't know about that," I say. "I do like to be alone, though."

I change the subject.

"Dad, I read on the Internet that you all used smoke grenades during the war. Will you tell me more about that?"

He is ready to talk. "Everyone carried smoke grenades. We had all kinds of colors. Red ones. Purple ones. Yellow ones. Blue ones. If a man in a helicopter was bringing supplies to us, he'd call us on the radio, ask us to pop one. That way he'd know exactly where we were. If you popped a yellow one, he might say, 'I see yellow. Is that you?' You'd say yes or no. Sometimes he'd say, 'I see two smoke grenades. Yellow and red.' You'd tell him you were the yellow and he'd open fire on the red. That was the enemy. He'd try to land then. He'd hover over top of us, drop everything down through the trees. He'd bring things like food, extra ammunition, clothing, mail. He'd drop a basket for mail, and for us to send old clothes back."

"What did they do with the old clothes? Wash them?" I ask. I'm really curious about this. It seems sort of odd to be worrying about old clothes in the middle of a war.

He pauses, has to think about the answer. "I don't know. Maybe burn them. We got a clean uniform every week, clean pants and shirt. I don't know if they were new ones or just clean ones. They sent clean socks once a week, too. I kept a lot of my socks, didn't send those back. I washed my own socks."

I'm amazed. I have never seen my father do laundry. My mother always took care of that sort of thing.

"How did you wash your socks?"

He clears his throat. His voice does not waver. "In a stream. I had one pair on, and a couple of pairs hung on my backpack. I kept C-rations in those socks. I've still got my can opener."

"What are C-rations?" I have to laugh at myself for being so curious about such small things when there are so many big things I know nothing about.

"Canned food. It's another name for it."

Now that he mentions it, I have seen C-rations before. My father was in the National Guard for a few years when I was in elementary school. How that happened is a story in itself. It seems that while he was going to the VA trying to get his disability, one of the doctors told him that he should join a veterans' organization. So one day while he and my mother were driving down the road he saw a group of men marching in front of a National Guard armory. For some reason he decided it was a veteran's organization. So he got out of the car right then and there and joined up. When he told the doctor about it on his next visit, the doctor was appalled. He said it was the worst thing my dad could have done and he might as well have jumped feet first into a fire. But by then it was too late. So when Dad came back from his two-week guard duty every year, he'd bring C-rations home and eat them. I tried some deviled ham once. It wasn't nearly as good as potted meat.

"What else do you have from the war, Dad?"

"Hammocks, boots, my uniform," he says. "I got a cane from Vietnam with a big dragon on the end that I gave to my dad when I got back. It was made of bamboo. When Dad died, Mom gave it back to me."

I get up and start walking around with the cordless phone, so excited that I can't sit still. "I remember that cane! I didn't know that was a dragon on the end. I thought it was the devil. I used to be afraid of it. Do you remember that?"

"No, I don't remember that. Wait. Yes, I do. You *were* afraid of it." He laughs.

"Would you give it to me?" I ask. I am serious. I want something of my father's to call my own, something to hold on to. I need that more and more these days.

"When I die, you can have it," he says matter-of-factly.

"Why can't I have it now?" I beg. "You could give it to me when I drop Mom off on Saturday."

He is not convinced. "I might need it. I'm getting old."

It hurts to hear this, though I'm sure he's kidding. "Stop saying that. You're not old. Did your dad really use it?"

"Dad used it. I have pictures of him using it."

"What was your dad like?" I ask hesitantly. My father's father has been dead for years, and I hope it's okay to bring him up.

"You don't remember him, Christal?" My dad sounds surprised.

"No, he died before I was born," I remind my father.

"He was a pretty old feller, I guess. He was like most of them Presley boys. He was a pretty good boy."

It's not enough. I want more. "What else about him?"

"He was just my dad." My father pauses. "I don't know what else to say."

"Were you close with him?" It's something I've always wondered about.

His voice is sad. "No, not really."

I try to lighten things up a bit. "Tell me about when you were a kid, and the animals you had."

"I had a dog. I had a pigeon that used to follow me to school. It would stay on top of the schoolhouse until I left, and then follow me home. That thing would light on my shoulder, follow me in the house. Its name was JoJo. That's what we called the monkey we had in Vietnam, too."

"What monkey?" I knew about the pigeon, but the monkey is news to me.

"We had a monkey in Vietnam called JoJo," he says.

"Where'd you all get a monkey?" I ask.

"Right in the jungle," he says, as if the answer should have been apparent. "One of those old boys got it from a village. It would ride on his back most of the time."

"What happened to it?"

"I don't know, Christal. I think the company commander found out and made him get rid of it."

There has to be more to it than that. "What do you mean, he had to get rid of it? What did he do with it?" I press.

"He gave it to one of the villagers. One of the Vietnamese. Some-one said they ate it. I don't know." My father's voice quivers. He doesn't want to talk about the monkey anymore. Without warning, he changes the subject. "Did Mom tell you they played my Vietnam song at Honaker High School on Veterans Day? They played it over the loudspeakers in the auditorium."

"No, she didn't," I say, taken by surprise. "You must have been really proud. Did anyone come up to you afterward and say anything about it?"

"No, they didn't know who I was. I sat there in the audience, but they didn't know it was me. Mommy should have stood up and hollered, 'That's my husband!' Shouldn't she have? What do you think? You tell her I said that, okay? Where is she now? Has Mommy gone to bed yet?"

"I think so." I pause. "What's your favorite memory as a child?" I ask him.

"I don't have any memories," he says, teasing me. "I don't remember when I was a child. I guess the day I was born I looked up at my mom and said, 'Who are you?'"

We both laugh. But I know he does remember some things.

"This cat is asleep on me right now. You should see it. It's curled up on my lap."

"Duma is asleep on me, too," I say. I look down at little Duma and smile as he opens his eyes and stretches before resting his head against my stomach and going back to sleep. Arthur is sprawled out on the floor next to my feet. When I make eye contact with him, he wags his tail.

"Dad, did you have any friends in your squad?" I ask, trying to get us back on track.

He sighs, his voice suddenly serious. "You don't get close to any-body. You don't get attached. You know what I mean?"

I am trying to understand, but I don't. "Not really," I say.

"Well, you didn't get attached to anybody; you didn't get close to anyone, because they died. They got killed. And you didn't want to get hurt."

"How can you not get attached to people?"

"You just don't. You train yourself."

I am not sure what to say next. I need to lighten the mood.

"Do you like talking to me on the phone, Dad?"

"Yes," he says at once.

I've never thought of my father as someone who likes to talk a lot. I never thought there was much he wanted to say. But he is certainly talking a lot now, and he said a lot at lunch the other day, too. I'm beginning to wonder if he's been wanting to talk all along, and I just didn't want to listen.

"Why do you like to talk to me?" I ask. I want to know what he thinks of me. I need to know that he likes me. But he's not taking the bait.

"I just like talking to you. Do *you* like talking to *me*, Christal?"

"Yes."

He laughs. "Wait till you get my bill. You'll change your mind."

Journal

On rare occasions when I was growing up, my father told stories about his childhood. He attended a one-room schoolhouse at the foot of the mountain, walking two miles to get there each day. He wore shoes only in the winter. The teacher sent him outside in the mornings to get lumps of coal for the stove.

For lunch, he ate out of a metal pail, sharing the meal with his siblings Millie, Lola, Junior, Ruth, and Gay. My father was the youngest of ten. The four eldest, Ernest, Elmer, Elden, and Jenelle, were already grown by then. Only Millie finished high school. Mamaw Presley said there was too much work to do at home to worry about getting a "book education."

My father spent evenings bringing water from the spring, hunting mushrooms and poke salad, scaring snakes with his firecrackers, all with his pet pigeon on his shoulder, while Mamaw tended the gardens and wrung chickens' necks for supper.

It sounded like a life right out of *Little House on the Prairie*. "There I am," he would holler, when he felt like coming out of his room and watching the series on television with me. "Behind that pigpen! In that tree! My big toe is sticking out of that creek! Do you see it?"

I sat on the floor as close to the TV as I could. If my father's big toe appeared on the screen, I didn't want to miss it.

He'd play his guitar during the commercials. "Sing along with me," he'd say.

I cannot think of my father without thinking of music. There was always music in the background. Ricky Skaggs. Ralph Stanley. Peter, Paul, and Mary. Especially Johnny Horton. War songs.

I wanted to get up and shake myself all over the place whenever I heard those songs. I didn't, though. Dancing like that would have been a sin.

Instead, Dad and I would sing along, so loud our eardrums hurt.

My favorite song was "Consider the Lilies." I wanted to be Candy Hemphill. My mother said she was a good Christian. I thought she was beautiful, and she had the voice of an angel.

I tried to make my voice sound like hers, turning one- and two-syllable words into three and four syllables.

My father laughed with delight at my attempts to imitate Candy. His whole face beamed.

"We could make it in Nashville," he said. "Me on the guitar and you on the vocals. Nashville's not gonna know what hit 'em."

Sometimes my mother would sing along, too, but he never told her she could make it in Nashville. He never asked her to go. I was always glad I had that. He saved Nashville for me.

So I guess there were some good memories after all.

Day Ten

"I had a nightmare today," I tell my father when I call this night. "It was when I took a nap after lunch."

Even thinking about that dream makes me nervous because I worry it means something bad is going to happen in my life. Specifically I'm worried about what my subconscious might have been trying to tell me about my relationship with Gurpreet.

I can hear my heart beating. I can't settle down. My mother is still with me, and since I woke up from my nap, I've been avoiding her. I want to be alone. I haven't told her about the dream. I want to tell my father. He's the one I want to confide in, yet I'm confused about these positive new feelings toward him. I'm not quite sure what to do with them. Feeling warmly about my father is just not within my comfort zone even though that was the purpose of these phone calls in the first place.

"What did you dream about?" he wants to know. He sounds concerned.

I start at the beginning.

In the dream, I sat in a Jeep. The top was down and the doors removed, the body outfitted with monstrous tires. A thick haze of dust settled in my throat. Dust, dust, everywhere.

I was in a deep pit of cracked and torn concrete. Had there been an earthquake? Where was I?

There was no one to ask.

Black high-rise buildings loomed all around, their windows like mirrors, my reflection in every one. I had to find Gurpreet. I needed Gurpreet. I was supposed to meet him, but I couldn't remember where. I cranked the Jeep and slammed on the gas, but I couldn't get out of that pit. No one to help me.

Suddenly, two men appeared. One was my friend Kevin. I don't remember the other.

They lifted the Jeep from the concrete ravine with nothing but their bare hands. They wanted to tell me something, but I was in a hurry.

"I have to meet Gurpreet," I told them. "Something is wrong. I have to find him."

I gunned the motor and didn't look back. I didn't even thank them. In the dream, I was crying.

It was then that I remembered—a parking garage. I was supposed to meet Gurpreet in a parking garage.

Next thing I knew, I was running through the garage, concrete on every side of me. I dashed up and down stairs, darted in and out of doors.

I had to find Gurpreet had to find Gurpreet had to find Gurpreet. Something was wrong. Terribly wrong. I had to get to him.

"Please! Someone help me!" I screamed.

No one was there.

I ran around for what seemed like hours, until I shook with sobs, until my legs gave way.

Gurpreet never came.

Drenched with sweat, my heart hammering all the way into my ears, I awoke from my nightmare.

My mouth was dry. Gurpreet. Water. Gurpreet.

I grabbed the phone, dialed his cell phone.

Please let him pick up, I prayed. I need to know that he's okay. *Please let him be okay.*

He is surprised to hear from me. It's midnight in Belgium. He has worked all day and will be back in Atlanta on Sunday.

"Are you okay?" he asks.

"I had a bad dream," I whisper.

Gurpreet is too exhausted to hear about my dream or to provide any emotional support. "Look, Christal, it's the middle of the night here," he says groggily. "I have to be up at six AM."

"Okay. I'm sorry," I say, apologetically, trying hard to hide my disappointment. "I'm sorry for waking you, and I love you."

"I love you, too," he says back. There is a gentle click on the other end.

I'm bothered by his hanging up so abruptly, but try to convince myself that I'm making a big deal out of nothing. It *is* the middle of the night, and Gurpreet has worked all day. Yes, the dream was upsetting, but I'm expecting too much if I think I can just unload on him whenever I feel like it.

I tell my father all about my nightmare, and leave out my phone conversation with Gurpreet. As I talk, I start to feel the tension draining from my body. It's amazing to me that talking to him actually has a calming effect on me.

"It was just a bad dream," he says reassuringly. "Just a dream. Sometimes we dream funny things."

Still, I have to wonder. I can't deny that things have been less than perfect between Gurpreet and me. Lately, we seem to be growing apart more than we're growing together, and I've had a sinking feeling about our relationship for some time.

"Do you ever have bad dreams?" I ask my father, pressing the phone tighter to my ear, trying to make him feel closer.

"I do sometimes," he says.

"About what?" I ask.

"About the service. About when I was in the war," he says softly.

"And is that what you tell yourself—that it's only a dream?" I ask.

"Yes."

"Does it work?"

"Whether it works or not, it's what you have to tell yourself," he says.

I don't know about that. Although I don't say anything, I'm wondering if maybe it's just another way to avoid acknowledging the truth.

• • •

Late that night, while my mother is sleeping, I look through several picture albums she's brought from home to give to me. The albums are arranged chronologically and labeled with the year and place they were taken.

She is right. I am smiling in most of them.

There is picture after picture of my father and me. In some of them, he holds me. In others, we hug. It looks natural, not the way we hug today.

Clearly there were happy times, but I still think of my childhood as a war zone, and I don't know how to change that.

When I reach age twelve, the pictures of my father and me together stop. We are separate after that, an invisible wall between us. I had reached the tipping point and pushed him as far away as I could. Retreating from him was the only way I knew to protect myself from the silent war being waged within our home. And in the end, even that didn't work.

Journal

Mae and Nancy Cox were sisters who went to my elementary school. Mae and I were both ten years old, and Nancy was eight. I felt a special connection with them, because one day, when no one was around, my mother had whispered, "Their father is like yours. I talked to Mrs. Cox about it once."

The "it," of course, was Vietnam. She didn't have to say it. The "it" was the way things were at home, my father's symptoms, how we walked on eggshells. I don't know how long they talked or what my mother told Mrs. Cox, but I latched on to that connection. I figured that if their father had been to Vietnam, their lives at home must be like mine. I became obsessed with being Mae and Nancy's friend.

But they weren't interested in being good friends. I was too odd, too unpredictable even for them.

"Why do your eyebrows do that?" Mae asked curiously. "Why do they raise up and down like that when you talk?"

"You're weird," Nancy told me. "Is there something wrong with you?"

After that, I locked myself in the school bathroom and cried. They hated me. What I needed was their understanding and acceptance, and they didn't give me that. No one ever did. Back then I was always on guard, ready for rejection, crying at the drop of a hat.

If a teacher said "good job," I cried because she didn't say "great." Good was not good enough. *I* was not good enough.

"Please sit up straight at your desk," another teacher said. I broke into tears.

My peers avoided me. "She's too sensitive," they said. "You can't say anything around her. Why is she so sensitive?"

What was the matter with me? Why couldn't I be like everyone else? Something was clearly wrong with my brain, I thought.

After a while I stopped trying and kept to myself. It was just easier that way.

Though I was very angry with my mother for not being able to change my father or protect me from him, I decided to find a way to make her my best friend. I longed for someone with whom I could share all my secrets the way best friends did, and she was the only person who knew the truth about the way we lived.

In my mind that meant she should also tell me everything about herself. I knew so little about her life. I knew she'd grown up in

Rowe, Virginia, the middle child of seven, and that she'd only got one spanking in her life. I knew her best friend when she was in high school was Dianna Hale. I knew she'd asked Jesus to save her when she was eleven, and she'd gotten the Holy Ghost and started speaking in tongues when she was twelve. At ten years old myself, that was all I knew, and I longed to know more.

I studied the autographs in my mother's senior yearbook and wondered what she was like as a young girl.

Good luck with L.J., some of the autographs read.

"Who is L.J.?" I asked my mother.

She didn't answer.

"Was he your boyfriend?" I asked.

Still nothing.

"What did you do back then? What did you talk about? What was on TV? Who is L.J.?"

"There was only your father," she said, not answering any question at all.

I threw myself to the ground and kicked and screamed, all to try to make her tell. But when I looked up to see if she was watching, she was already gone. My father was in the middle of yet another episode and had locked himself in his room. No tantrum I threw was going to top that.

Day Eleven

My mother says my father is in a good mood today. She's talked to him twice already. She is at peace, relaxed, and comfortable as I drive her back to Knoxville to meet him.

When my father is in a good mood, my mother gives herself permission to be happy. When his mood changes, so does hers. Sometimes I want to throttle her for allowing him to dictate her moods, but then I realize that it had been the same for me when we were all living under one roof.

"He sounded so cheerful," she reminds me again, as she smiles and looks out the window.

It is a good day, and she's glad to be going home. Being in the same house with me for seven days straight has been a lot to handle. I know she's confused by my increasing concern for and allegiance to my father, and she's not sure what to do now that she can no longer count on me to be her ally against my dad. Truthfully, I'm confused myself. I'm still not comfortable with these shifting alliances. My mother needs help, but I'm no longer willing to be her sole emotional support and keeper of her secrets. I can't keep living a lie. I'd told her this point-blank earlier in the week. I have to acknowledge the truth about what happened to me when I was a child. Otherwise, I'll never be able to process it. I'll never be able to move past it. My own health and well-being are more important than keeping secrets.

I wonder now if my mother truly understands the seriousness of what we endured back then.

"Do you think you'd want to go to counseling?" I ask as we're driving.

"I don't know if I need it," she says, still staring out the window. Therapy is something I've mentioned to her before, and her response is always the same.

I bite my lip. I want to shake some sense into her, tell her how wrong she is. But I keep my mouth shut because I know it won't do any good, and it might even start an argument.

When we meet at the designated gas station, my father and I share an awkward hug. I have been worried about this, how it would be when I saw him again. I didn't want to get my hopes up. Things can still turn on a dime.

He walks to his car and hands me several thick hardcover books from the passenger seat. "Here," he says. "I don't need these, but you might."

I recognize them immediately. They're the encyclopedias about Vietnam that I got him for Christmas last year.

He's right. I do need them now. As I put them in my car, I notice that on the cover of the top one there's a photograph of several young soldiers crouched in a deep trench. I don't know much about the war, but I know they're in a foxhole. I make a mental note to ask my father about foxholes as soon as I have a chance.

At lunch he is full of jokes and says he's going to leave my mother with me for another seven days to see how I like that.

He knows how fretful she can be, and he loves to tease her just to see if he can get a rise out of her.

She forces a smile and shakes her head. She's ready to go back to Honaker, and I'm ready for her to go.

"Are you ever going to come visit me in Atlanta?" I ask him.

"No," he says. "I have to stay home with the cat and dog."

Mom jumps in as usual. "I've told you I'd stay home with them and you could go back with Christal," she says.

"Maybe someday," he says, and changes the subject.

My father tells us he left home at 5:00 this morning—almost three hours before he had to. He likes to drive around by himself, explore little dirt roads, get off the beaten path. I like that, too.

"I bought two hats at the flea market," he tells us. The hats have "USA" embroidered on them in red, white, and blue. He says he stopped at the flea market on the way here to get them.

"I didn't know you still wore hats," I say.

"Not for me," he says. "For two friends."

I am shocked. "Music buddies?" I ask.

"No," he says. "Other friends."

"I didn't know you had friends," I say, "other than the guys you used to play music with, I mean."

"Two old boys from Council, Virginia," he says. "They're veterans, too. Fought in Vietnam. Not in my company though. One is eat up with cancer. I'll bet he doesn't weigh a hundred pounds."

"Was it Agent Orange?" I ask.

He looks down, nods. "Lung cancer."

I wonder if he's thinking about the mass he had removed from his own lung. The doctors thought that was Agent Orange, too.

"Dad, did you ever dig foxholes?" I ask, changing the subject. Thinking about Agent Orange and my father hooked up to so many tubes when he had his mass removed is too painful to dwell on for long.

"Dug them everywhere," he says. "Wherever you went, you dug a foxhole. Every night you dug a sleeping quarter, too. That is, if you wasn't sleeping in a hammock in the trees. A foxhole is deeper than the place where you'd dig to sleep at night. You had to crouch down in a foxhole and hide. If you dug your sleeping quarter right, it wasn't as deep, but it was wider than a foxhole. You could stretch out in it. Digging. We was always digging. When we weren't digging, we was pulling the leeches off of us."

I cringe just to think what that must have been like.

"We would wake up and leeches would be all over us. You'd no sooner pull one off than it'd grab on to you in another place."

"How did you get them off?"

"If you smoked, you'd burn them off with your cigarette or your lighter," he says. "Me—I used bug juice." He explains that "bug juice" is what the soldiers in his division called the insecticide they were given to use. "I sprayed it on those leeches, and they fell right off," he says, sounding pleased with himself.

My father has eaten today. I've watched him carefully. He's not nervous like the last time. His voice is strong and steady. He asks for a box for our leftover food, piles every crumb from all our plates inside. He'll eat this later. If he doesn't, he'll give it to his dog.

Time passes quickly. We talk a little more, looking at our watches, and decide we all need to get home. We have animals to feed and things to do.

I hug my mother and my father. The gesture seems more natural with my father now, and more forced with my mother. I feel a strange mixture of pity and relief as she walks away.

I am pulling out of the parking lot when my father flags me down and motions for me to open my window.

"Don't forget to call me tomorrow," he says excitedly. "I *want* you to call me."

Journal

When I was a child, there were many opportunities to say something about my father's condition and its effects on my family. There were a few kids with whom I played basketball and softball. There were neighbors. I saw my extended family often. But I was never really close to any of them. I never said a word about any of it—my father's depression, his withdrawal, his rages, or my mother's silence.

I always planned to say something, thought it all out in my head, envisioned myself many times flinging open the doors of truth, finally emerging from the darkness. But I never did. What if no one believed me?

People would judge me and call me a liar. I'd be ruined.

Or what if they *did* believe me?

Then they would judge my parents, and I'd be responsible.

My parents were upstanding members of the church. In our world, one had to be perfect in order to reach heaven. A single unforgiven sin would send a person straight to the depths of hell.

Telling the truth about what my life was really like would mean exposing my parents as less than perfect. I loved them too much for that. Telling the truth would mean exposing myself, too. What if I was to blame for my father's behavior? There had to be something wrong with me. Otherwise, he'd want to get close.

I couldn't run the risk that my peers—my neighbors—my extended family—wouldn't understand. *I* did not understand.

No place felt safe. No place in the world.

I needed help. We all needed help, but there was no one to help us.

So I kept quiet, my hands clamped hard around our lives so nothing would escape through the cracks.

Day Twelve

"You need to go down to the VA hospital sometime. Atlanta has one," my father says.

That's the last place I want to go. I have bad memories of VA hospitals. I went with my father to the one in Johnson City, Tennessee, a few times when I was eight. I went inside twice. That was enough. The other times I waited in the car—locked myself inside, and monitored the perimeter with my dad's binoculars. If someone came too close, I hid on the floor.

For years, I dreamed of crazy, open-mouthed men, saliva dripping from their chins, their arms reaching for me. The ones with no legs chased after me in their wheelchairs.

"Go look sometime," my father says, again, interrupting my thoughts. "You'll see people with no arms, no legs. People who came back from the war. Some are brain damaged."

He doesn't have to tell me. I remember all too well.

Years ago, during the times when my father was at his worst, he'd tell my mother and me that he was going to the VA hospital to live.

He'd curl into a ball, rock back and forth, and tears would roll down his face. There was no consoling him when he was like that, and my mother didn't even dare to try because she knew that his tears could easily turn to fury. And if they did, we'd both bear the brunt of his verbal abuse. Also, when my father was angry, he was more likely to get one of his guns and head for the river.

He never once threatened to use the gun on my mother or me, but his actions were so frequently extreme and irrational—and his mood changes so quick and unpredictable—that we both feared there was a chance he would kill us some day. And, of course, each time he went to the river we were afraid he'd never return.

There were times when I prayed he would pack his bags and leave, just go. Go and never come back. Maybe we could be normal then, just my mother and me.

Yet I knew that I'd die if he left. I could not live without him, could not go on.

I had it all planned. If he ever tried to move out, I'd fling myself on the floor, grab onto his legs, and hold on until the police pulled me off. I'd bite them on the fingers, kick and scream, and cause such a ruckus they wouldn't know what hit them. We'd all leave together then—all three of us. Start over. Never come back to this place.

He was not leaving without me.

Thinking about VA hospitals now brings it all back. Am I ready for that? I've come this far, but I'm still not sure.

"Would I be able to go in?" I ask my father, half hoping he'll say no. "I don't think I could get in."

"You can get in," he says. "It's just like a regular hospital. You can go in and walk around. . . . Look in the phone book," he says, "or on the Internet. You can get an address."

Even thinking about going inside the VA makes me nervous. I want to talk about something else, and I change the subject.

"How high up did you tie your hammocks in the trees?" I ask. I've been looking at pictures of hammocks in one of the encyclopedias on Vietnam.

"High enough so your rear didn't touch the ground. If you tied them too high, you couldn't get in them. We had ponchos, too. We'd tie them above the hammocks for when it rained."

"Who was your sergeant? Your lieutenant?" I ask. The encyclopedias say that each squad had a sergeant. Each platoon had a lieutenant. Each company had a captain. I sound like I know a little something now. I feel good about that, however minimal it is.

"I don't remember all those old boys," my father says. "There were so many. Always coming and going. Always dying. Then someone new would show up. I can't keep up with their names anymore."

He tells me he was in Vietnam for a year. The *Freedom Bird* came to get him after that. This was what "all those old boys" called the plane that took them back to the States, far away from the war.

"Did women fight in Vietnam?" I ask.

"I don't remember any women soldiers," my father says. "But there were women nurses. One nurse got killed. A rocket hit a wing of the hospital and killed her. She was the only American woman killed in Vietnam. At least, I think that's right."

"Did you all talk to each other during the day when you were in the field, Dad?"

I imagine my father, a young and slender man, like I have seen in the pictures. He is crouched low to the ground, moving forward with the rest of his squad. They walk in a line, follow a path. Their hands are on their guns. Always ready. Blades of grass as high as their thighs sway in the breeze. There is jungle left and right. When the jungle ends there are rice paddies that stretch as far as the eye can see. The air smells of smoke.

"We whispered sometimes," he says. "More than anything, we used hand signals."

"What kind of booby traps did you see?" I ask. I'm really getting into this now.

"Lord, so many. You are going to have to look them up in those encyclopedias. They'll have pictures there, too. I can't describe them. One kind of booby trap was punji stakes. Look that up, too."

"What are they?"

"Snipers would shoot, so you'd jump off the trail," he says. "You'd jump right in those big pits. At the bottom were punji stakes—big, thick sticks sharpened to a point. Sometimes the Vietnamese would put their own feces on the tips. Those stakes would rip right through you if you fell in there. If you lived through that, you'd get gangrene afterward. Lots of soldiers lost their legs because of those traps."

My stomach turns. Imagining such pain and suffering reminds me of the pictures I saw of the My Lai massacre during the class on Vietnam I took when I was in college.

I've been reading about My Lai in the encyclopedias my father returned to me, and what happened there doesn't make sense. It sounds like there were rumors of enemy soldiers hiding in one particular village. Orders were given to wipe it out. It was a farming village, like many in Vietnam. Most of the men were gone that day. It was the women and children who were at home when the troops came in.

Was my father there? Is this what he was talking about when he said he'd done things he regrets?

I want to ask. I need to understand.

"Were you in My Lai, Dad?"

"Not during the massacre," he replies quickly. "I was asked to pull guard there while some men from the Pentagon flew in. They asked the villagers where all the graves were and what happened in that place. Guess they were trying to figure out if the rumors were true. I was one of the old boys pulling guard while they dug up all the bodies."

"I read about that," I say, confident for once that I have something to contribute to the conversation. "There were 500 bodies," I announce, so sure of myself.

"You are wrong about that," he says suddenly. "There were 504."

My jaw drops. He knows the exact number. But of course he would; he was there when they were dug up. I can't imagine what that must have been like, and I don't have the courage to ask. I'm relieved when my father tells me my mother wants to talk to me.

"Do you think when all this is over, you'll remember all the good things?" she wants to know. She sounds worried.

I wish she'd stop asking questions like that. "I hope so," I reply. I've already started remembering some positive times, but her pressing me just makes me not want to admit it to her.

"I sent another picture to you," she says. "I have more pictures here. There are so many of them."

When I bought a new computer a few years ago, I gave the old one to my mother. She'd gone out and bought herself a scanner, learned how to scan in her old photos, and learned how to e-mail them to me. It was sometimes amazing to me how smart and independent she could be about everything else and still be so timid and terrified when it came to dealing with Dad.

I open the picture on my computer. I am thirteen. Smiling.

You should remember how happy you were, I know she wants to say.

I shake my head and close my eyes.

She puts my father back on. I try to be cheery, but I don't feel cheery. Between my day job, this project with my father, and putting the finishing touches on my dissertation, I'm just exhausted all the time. And I'm also coming to realize that no matter how hard I try, I will never be able to truly wrap my head around what my father saw and experienced in the war. That makes me sad and more than a little guilty, because it also makes me realize how much worse it was than I could ever have imagined.

"I defend my dissertation next week," I tell him. "You know, that big, long paper I wrote this year."

"You can buy me a good Christmas present this year, then. You can buy me a CF Martin guitar." He laughs. "So, what can I call you next week? Doctor?"

"I guess," I say.

"Doctor Christal Presley," he says. His voice is proud. He likes the sound of it.

"Doctor of what?" he wants to know.

"Education," I say. I need to talk to my father tonight more than usual. I don't know why, but I do. So, to prolong the conversation I ask, "Dad, what do you remember about me as a child?"

"I don't remember much," he replies. "Except you were as mean as you could be."

"I was mean?" I ask, truly shocked.

He laughs. Then I realize he is kidding. "You weren't mean, honey," he says soothingly.

"I remember we used to go fishing," he says, more serious now. "Don't you remember?"

"I do remember that," I say. "What else do you remember?"

"That's about it." There is a pause. He is thinking. "Well, you used to want to be a horse. You'd see horses outside, roll down the window and neigh, and the horses would come running. Do you remember that?"

"Sort of."

"And you loved dogs. Lord, you loved your dogs. You'd do anything for those dogs."

He's right. I did. Some things will never change.

I want to ask more. I want him to help me remember, and I also want to know what he was thinking back then.

"Did you think I would be affected by the war?" I hold my breath. I worry about how he will respond.

"No, I didn't think you would be. Are you? How did you get affected? You weren't there."

I can't believe he really doesn't know. But if he really doesn't, I can't tell him how it was for me back then. Not tonight. I'm afraid he won't be able to handle it. It isn't time. Maybe it never will be.

I'm glad when he doesn't wait for an answer.

"Christal, they had tunnels in Vietnam. Tunnels under the ground. They'd put booby traps in there, poisonous snakes. Some of the Vietnamese lived down there. They used those tunnels to hide or to get from one place to another in secret. Those tunnels were hard to find. They'd hide them good, put bamboo over them. We used to have to send men down there to check the tunnels out. We called them fellers 'tunnel rats.' I never went down there, just stuck my head in."

"I was too big," he says. "Too big and ugly." He laughs a little, waits for me to laugh, too.

I don't. I am feeling serious tonight.

"If you could give any advice to families of veterans, Dad, what would you tell them?"

"I don't know," he says.

"You have to know *something*, Dad."

His voice quivers. I am pressing his limit. "They need to find a group to get in and get counseling," he says.

"Why do you think they need counseling?" I am not letting up now. I need to hear him say that he values counseling as a way to help people sort out their problems.

"Either that, or go jump off a cliff," he says indifferently.

I cringe at the very idea that my father can mention suicide so casually.

"They need to go to counseling before those veterans get back from the war," he says. "So they know what to expect."

"What *should* they expect, Dad?" I need to know.

"War changes a person."

"How?"

"It just changes people. You . . . it . . . it just changes people. I can't explain it."

"Do you think it changes families?"

"It changes everything."

I think back to the question my father just asked about how I could be affected by a war I wasn't even in. He is contradicting himself. I wonder if he realizes more than he's willing to acknowledge about how Vietnam affected my mother and me.

"I'm going to visit the veterans' hospital here," I tell him. I've decided to take his advice. I think that maybe I *should* see how other veterans are doing. At least I might find out why he's so adamant about my needing to go.

"Is it close?" he says.

"It's not too far."

"You need to do that," he says again.

"Why do you want me to go there, Dad?"

"I just want you to go," he says. "I want you to appreciate what you've got, what these boys do."

He clears his throat. "Tell them I sent you," he says.

I want to end on a positive note. We've gone deeper tonight than ever before.

"Tell me something good you did today," I say. "Something fun."

"It weren't much fun," he says. "But I took Mommy out and bought her some food. She owes me next time. This old feller believes in equal rights."

He is okay now; his voice is back to normal. He's made a joke. It is a good night, and my father is well.

Journal

"Where did you get JoJo the pigeon?" I would ask whenever I was sure my father was in a good mood and when I had him all to myself.

I loved hearing him tell this story over and over again.

"JoJo just showed up one day," he would say. "Showed up and lit on my shoulder. I started feeding him and he stayed."

Then I'd ask, "How did you know he was a boy?"

My father would squirm and say, "Just knew."

"No, really. How did you know?" I'd urge. "Tell me, Dad. Tell me."

"Why, he told me so!" my father would exclaim and slap his hand against his knee for effect. "He lit on my shoulder and said, 'Hi, my name is JoJo, and I'm a boy. It's nice to meet you. I'll be staying with you for a while.'"

He'd say JoJo's words in a squeaky voice that would make me cackle.

"Do it again, Dad! Say what JoJo said again!"

He'd fold his arms against his chest and shake his head. Stubborn as could be, my father. "No," he'd tell me. "Only once."

I'd have to wait until another day when he told the story again to hear him talk like that.

"What happened to him, Dad? What happened to JoJo?"

"JoJo stayed for years," he would say, before his voice became more somber. "Then he flew away one day, pretty as you please. I guess he couldn't take being around me anymore."

His smile would disappear then, his eyes suddenly distant.

"He never did come back," he'd say.

I'd try to change the subject then and get him to tell me about something else, always hoping but never daring to ask, that he'd tell a story about the war.

He did have other stories, but none of them was ever about the war. The only story about the war I ever heard was from a buddy of his, Earl Casey.

Earl was one of the few friends my father ever had, and I couldn't have been more than ten when he told me a story Dad had once told him.

Earl and my father used to play music together. Earl on the piano and my father on the guitar, and you'd have thought they came straight from Nashville.

"Your father's been through it," Earl said to me one day when my father had left the room. The comment came out of nowhere, and I still have no idea what might have precipitated it.

"He told me he was always going in and out of villages when he was in Vietnam. Mostly, there were only women and children there. Sometimes you had to follow orders and do things you didn't want to do, kill people you didn't want to kill. You didn't just kill soldiers. You know what that means, don't you?"

I felt faint. Why was he telling me this?

"Your father said those women and children were crying and talking in a different language, but he knew what they were saying," Earl continued. "Something like that would mess you up forever."

I sat huddled on the sofa for the rest of the night, pulling my legs tightly into my chest, as I stared at my father strumming on his guitar. I must have known that he'd killed people, but until then I'd just assumed they were Vietnamese soldiers. What Earl told me was horrifying, and instead of making me feel more sympathetic toward my father, it just disgusted me.

My nightmares started after that. They were always the same, and they came a few times a week.

My father was young, like the man in the pictures on the wall upstairs. His look was sad and serious, and he was walking through what I imagined to be the jungles of Vietnam. He zigzagged through the tall grass, kept low to the ground. All night long in my dream he walked, alone and by the moonlight.

Many times I yelled out to him, to signal that I was there so that he would stop and wait for me. And each time he would turn around to look. He seemed confused. His eyes were old. He could not see me.

Even though Earl's story horrified me, I was jealous of him—not because of *what* he told me, but because my father had chosen to tell him and not me. I began to despise Earl after that because he was the "chosen one." Then, over the years, I began to realize how inappropriate it would have been for my father to tell a story like that to a little girl, and I started to hate Earl even more for having told it to me.

Day Thirteen

I talk to my mother first tonight. She's been on my mind all day. She came up in my therapy session today way more than my father did. I need to make sure she's okay, that she knows I don't blame her for what my father did when I was a child. I need her to know that I love her and that I realize she was a victim, too. I tell her all these things. I need her to know that I am trying to understand.

"I *was* a good mother," my mother says. She needs validation tonight.

"You were," I say, truthfully. "And you *are*." It's taken a lot of years and a lot of therapy, but finally I really do understand that she and Dad did the best they could with what they had and what they knew.

I also want to make sure she doesn't feel left out. It's been a long time since my father and I have had any kind of relationship. This will take some getting used to for everyone.

My conversation with my father is short.

"Hey, buddy," he says when he gets on the phone. He has never called me "buddy" before. I feel warm and tingly inside, like a little girl all over again.

"Hi, buddy," I say. It feels weird, but I like it.

I want to know more about my childhood. I want to know his favorite memory of me.

"I don't know," he says, pondering the question seriously. "Everything."

I need something specific. "Tell me one thing," I say. "One favorite memory of me."

"I remember when you caught your first fish," he says, happy to have come up with something.

"Really?" I ask. "How big was it?" I don't remember this particular fishing trip.

"Forty pounds," he says. I can almost see him grinning.

"Dad, no it wasn't. Tell me the truth."

"It was a little bitty fish," he says. "Don't you remember?"

I wish I did. I wish someone could open up my head and put the memory back in.

My therapist says that my not remembering the good things isn't that uncommon, given my situation. "Sometimes the bad things overshadow the good" is the way that she'd put it.

"Tell me about the day I was born," I say to my father. I want to build more memories—good ones—even if they aren't my own for now. I want to know how things were for him back then, what he thought of me that day.

He pauses, sighs. "I don't remember," he says.

I wasn't expecting this. I'm shocked and disappointed.

"But how can you not remember the day I was born? You were there, weren't you?"

"There in the hospital, but not in the room when Mommy had you," he says. "They didn't let men go in back then."

"What did you think of me when you saw me?" I ask with some anticipation.

Another pause. "I don't remember that day," he says glumly. "They say you made a face at me when you saw me through the glass. You didn't like me much even back then. Don't you remember that?"

"You know I don't," I say.

"Well, I don't remember things either," he says.

"Why don't you remember?" I want to know.

His voice is quiet. "I don't remember a lot of things," he says. "After the war . . ." His voice trails off in silence.

I realize then that this is one of the things that scares me most, that I, too, will never be able to retrieve my memories, that my mind will always be a dark cloud, that I will always remember more bad than good.

Journal

My father couldn't have forgotten the war even if he'd wanted to. My mother wouldn't let him.

She polished the old army boots he'd hidden outside in the storage shed and told her to throw away. Then she put them in a glass shadowbox and gave them to him for his birthday. It was the boots one birthday, his army hat the next, then his war medals lined up in a row. It was black-and-white pictures of him in uniform, American flags on sticks, his dog tags, the little Bible the army gave him—all worn and raggedy. Each item was preserved in a glass case my mother said I was never to touch. There were compasses and angle-headed flashlights, sweat towels and poncho liners, and posters of eagles in flight.

War, my parents' bedroom screamed.

I was afraid of it.

But sure enough, that was the room where my father locked himself up whenever he got too depressed to deal with everyday life.

Stretched flat on the floor like a snake, I'd press my face into the blue shag carpet and try to spy through the crack at the bottom of the door. Flickers of light and dark emerged from within.

A voice that sounded important said, "At this moment, our brave servicemen and women stand watch in that distant desert and on distant seas, side by side with the forces of more than twenty other nations. They are some of the finest men and women of the United States of America. And they're doing one terrific job."

This was in 1990, during Desert Storm. It was the first major military conflict the United States had engaged in since Vietnam. It brought back memories for my father with a vengeance.

I wanted to knock, burst right in, claw my way through the door, because I knew he was in there with his arms folded tight around his waist, his body rocking back and forth. I wanted to help. But I couldn't do it. I was too scared.

My mother paced from the kitchen to the hallway to the locked door and back. She knew better than to go in there when he got like this. There was no telling if her words or her mere presence would set him off and be the catalyst for a trip to the river with his gun.

Day Fourteen

There are lots of things I have inherited from my father: his eyes, his wrinkled forehead, his nervous energy. We are both hyper-aware of our surroundings, of people's body language, of verbal and nonverbal cues. We stand back and skim the crowd, look for exits before we enter a room, and are never first or last because it is safer to be in the middle. We are private, reserved. We do not trust easily. My father got that way from being in Vietnam, and I got it from being around him.

We listen before we speak. We can tell in an instant whether people are being sincere.

This scares some people.

"I got a nativity scene today of baby Jesus," my mother says tonight. "Dad fixed a spotlight on it for me. It looks good in the dark."

She talks about the cat named Avery. He will eat only one particular kind of food, canned not dry.

"Should I keep buying it for him?" she wants to know. "I know I'm spoiling him." She tells me about his litter-box habits and how shiny his hair is.

My father tells me about his day. He and my mother took Mamaw Shortridge, my mother's mother, to the store. They went to the Golden Corral for lunch. My father likes buffets because he believes this is the best way to get his money's worth.

"We had dead fish and dead chicken," he says. "It was pretty good. Would have been better if Mommy or Mamaw Shortridge had paid."

I laugh at my father's joke.

"What caused the Vietnam War, Dad?" I want to know. I want to ask about the war tonight, so I feel him out a little to see if it's okay. If he seems uncomfortable, we don't have to stay there. We can always talk about something else.

"I don't know," he says after a moment.

"Do you know why you were fighting?"

"No, I don't," he says. "I think the people in the North were trying to take over the South. We were helping South Vietnam, trying to keep the North from taking over."

"Why did it matter if the North took over the South?" I ask.

"The North was communist. The South was capitalist," he replies matter-of-factly.

"What would that have meant for the U.S.—if the North took over the South, I mean?"

"I don't know," he says. "After we left, North Vietnam took over South Vietnam anyway. Now it's just one Vietnam. I still don't understand. I don't know what they were fighting for. I don't know why we

went there." He pauses, then asks, "Did you read in those encyclopedias about Kent State?"

"No. What's Kent State?"

"It was a college campus," he says. "Students were protesting. The
National Guard went in and shot some of them. It happened in Ohio.
You'll have to read about it. I seen it on TV when I came out of the
war. When I came out of Vietnam, they were lined up at the airport.
The American people hated us."

"How did you feel about that?" I ask tentatively.

"You feel like a rotten dog. You'd like to get some of them and
hang them. For a long time I wouldn't even tell people I'd been in
service. It was just bad," he goes on. "Some boys left and went to
Canada. They dodged the draft. The U.S. couldn't get them."

"Did you ever think about going to Canada?"

"I wouldn't disgrace my parents like that," he says.

"How would that have been a disgrace to them?" I ask.

"Dad was proud of me for going into the service. I didn't want
Dad to have to explain to people that he had a boy that refused to
serve his country. . . . Are *you* proud I went to service?" he asks me.

That takes me by surprise. I'm the one who's supposed to be asking the questions. "I don't know," I answer. What else am I supposed
to say?

"What do you mean, you 'don't know'?" he asks, a bit taken aback.

"I . . . I've never thought about it before," I reply. "I'm just sorry
you had to go through what you did." I pause. "Are *you* proud you
went, Dad?"

"Don't know if I'm proud, but I'm glad for you and Mommy that
I went. If something happens to me, Mommy will be taken care of.

You got your college free because of it. They pay for Mommy's medication for her Parkinson's. But I hate that I have those dreams I do. I just hate those old war dreams."

I remember the thick pads on which my father used to sleep. The VA sent them to soak up the sweat from those dreams. He calls them war dreams, but no doubt they were actually nightmares.

"Did Mommy tell you they played my song on the loudspeakers at the high school? On Veterans Day?"

He wants to talk about something else. He has had enough of the war for tonight.

"*You* told me that."

"Do you think she was proud of me?" he wants to know.

"Of course she was. I'm proud of you, too."

"What do you think about my song?"

"I love it."

"Have you listened to it?"

"Yes."

"How many times?"

"A bunch."

I'd had his CDs for a long time, but I hadn't ever played them until we started these conversations. He'd written a song about Vietnam that I played over and over, especially after one of our conversations. It made me sad to hear the hurt in his voice as he sang it. But as we grew closer, it was also comforting to hear his voice, as if a part of him were in the house with me.

"How is your friend doing, Dad? The veteran with cancer?"

"I call him every other day. Some days he's okay, and some days he's not. He ain't gonna make it too much longer. I went to school with that old boy."

His voice trails off. He is distant now, his mind somewhere else. "The Agent Orange got that old boy," he says.

I still don't know what to do when he gets like this. What do I say? Will it make a difference?

We both pull away, say our good-byes.

I tell him I'll call him tomorrow.

As soon as I put down the phone, I call back. I have forgotten something.

"Yes?" he says. He is watching the caller ID. The numbers are programmed to come up on the TV screen.

"I forgot to tell you something," I say.

"What is it?"

Now is my chance.

"Thank you for serving your country, Dad." It is the first time I have ever thanked my father for fighting in Vietnam.

There is a silence between us, as if he is speechless. "Thank you, honey, for saying that," he says after a while.

My mother calls back about an hour later.

"I'm proud of you. So proud," she says. "I'm glad you said what you did to your father." Her voice is stronger than I've heard in months. Her words are so light they float. "You should hear him upstairs playing that guitar tonight," she continues. "It's like nothing you have ever heard. . . ."

Journal

I remember one particular fishing trip I took with my father when I was nine. We went to Little River, a twenty-minute drive on narrow dirt roads. We dug our own night crawlers from under a shade tree. I could hardly wait to bait my hook and throw my line into the water!

The river ran through the middle of a pasture. Black cattle gathered in clusters at the water's edge, sticking out their long tongues to lap the water. There was a single brick silo in the distance that my father warned me not to go near.

"It's dangerous," he said. "Old as the hills."

Though I was curious about the silo, even from a distance it looked like it was crumbling. I could see why he thought it was dangerous.

He let me put the worm on the hook myself. I cast the line as far as I could throw it and waited. It wasn't long before I felt a tug.

"Look, Dad! Look! I beat you! I beat you! I caught the first fish!" I shrieked excitedly, jumping up and down as it dangled from my line.

But my excitement quickly turned into tears. I couldn't remove the hook, couldn't throw the fish back into the water. It had swallowed hook and worm whole, and now it lay dying in my hands. Blood began to seep through its gills and onto my fingers.

"Help her, Dad! She's dying!" I shrieked, convinced it was a girl.

My father rushed over and took her from me. He tugged gently on the line.

"She's dying!" I howled.

"Shhhh," my father said. He was calm, collected, and confident. His hands did not shake. "It'll be okay. When they swallow the hook, you can sometimes tug it free. But don't jerk too hard. You'll rip the guts out. The fish won't live if you rip the guts out."

He pulled lightly on the twine again. More blood oozed from the gills.

"Please, oh please, don't pull it anymore! You're going to kill her! You're going to kill her!" I was practically hyperventilating.

Still cupped in his hands, my father tenderly submerged the fish in the water, and tilted her with her tail down and her mouth up.

"So she can get more oxygen," he said. When he looked at me that day, he didn't look old or worn.

The fish lurched from side to side. It was impossible to tell whether his efforts were hurting or helping.

"If the hook doesn't come out when you tug it, then don't worry," my father said. "You can cut the line."

Tears dripped down my cheeks.

"Shhhhh," he said. "It's okay. The hook and line will dissolve, even if they're left inside the fish. That's the good thing. They're made that way."

At that, he took his pliers and cut the line in two. He freed her.

She stayed near the surface for just an instant, still struggling. Then, as if by some miraculous force, she realized she was no longer a prisoner and dove into the depths.

"Will she be okay?" I asked my father, chewing the sides of my nails as I spoke. "I don't think she's going to make it."

"She'll be fine," he said. "Know how I know?"

My eyes stung. I had my doubts. "How do you know?"

"She didn't roll over on her side and float to the top. She plunged right in. She didn't stop fighting. It's ones like that that always make it," he said.

We fished until the sun set that evening, laughing and joking with each other, keeping a constant count of who'd caught the most fish. The competition was close—and ever-changing. In the end, I beat my father by a single fish. The last thing I remember us doing that day is walking side by side through the pasture, our fishing poles slung over our shoulders, the tall grass rubbing against my knees. My father was happy and calm.

For a long time I didn't remember that day. Probably I didn't want to. I'd been so angry with him for so long that the bad things were all that I thought of. It's interesting how the good memories come back when you stop being angry.

Day Fifteen

M y mother is not well. I can tell at once.

"What's wrong?" I ask, although I already know.

"I don't know what to tell you," she says. "I can't move. My whole body can't move. The medication is wearing off."

"Can you take more medication?" I ask.

I wish I could be closer, yet I'm glad I'm far away. It's hard to see her like this. It's bad enough imagining it.

"I did. It's just one of those things," she says. She sighs. "My body's gotten used to this medication. It doesn't work so well now, even when I take more."

She's had Parkinson's for seven years now, but it's only been three years since she's spoken about it openly. Before that, the only people who knew were my father and me and a few select family members. She and I have both always been good at keeping secrets. But now the whole family knows, as well as the members of my parents' church.

Even now, it's hard for me to talk about her illness. I'd rather push it to the side and pretend she's fine. She's just having a bad day. Tomorrow will be better.

"What would you think if I took a trip to Vietnam in a few months?" I ask her. It's something I've only started to think about in the last couple of days, and the first time I've spoken about it to anyone. I've found an organization online called Soldier's Heart that organizes retreats throughout the United States for veterans and their family members coping with PTSD, as well as trips to Vietnam for veterans and their children.

"Oh, my Lord. Wouldn't that be dangerous? Why do you want to go there?" She is clearly troubled by this idea.

"To see . . . ," I say, but don't finish the sentence. I haven't figured it all out yet myself.

"How many miles away is Vietnam?" she asks, her voice becoming increasingly agitated.

"I don't know," I answer.

"It's all the way on the other side of the world, isn't it?" She does not try to hide her anxiety.

"Yes," I tell her. I am hesitant to talk about it anymore because she already sounds so fretful. The last thing I want is to upset her, or for her to try to influence my decision.

I suddenly hear my father in the background and am grateful for the opportunity to end this conversation. He is itching to get on the phone with me.

"Is that Christal? It's Christal, isn't it?" I hear him say.

"I appreciate you calling." It's the first thing he tells me when my mother hands him the phone.

He has a host of questions of his own today. Who works in my office? Do I have a room to myself? How often am I there? What is my job? What does it mean to be a mentor of teachers? How many schools do I go to? What are the kids like in Atlanta? Do I see any homeless people? Are any of them veterans? But he doesn't wait for my answers.

"I would never find my way around down there," he says. "They'd send me to a school and I'd end up in Florida. You can drive down there. I couldn't. I can't concentrate. Not in traffic."

He's right about that, but I do not say it. I don't ever want to discourage him from coming here, but driving will not be an option. He'd have a breakdown in the traffic here and cause my mother to have one of her own if she came with him. I'd probably have one of my own just thinking about them both on Interstate 75.

My father refuses to fly. He hasn't flown since the war. If he ever came to visit, I'd have to go get him—and take him back.

"Mommy is going to call the DMV," he says. "She says they need to take away my license. She says I can't drive a lick. Do you think I'm that bad?"

I grimace. "Pretty bad," I say. The truth is, it's been years since I've ridden in a car with him because I'm scared out of my mind to do it. I assume his driving habits haven't changed. As a kid I was always praying, holding on to the door handle, closing my eyes so I didn't have to look.

I don't like to think negative things, but I keep waiting for him to have an accident and have his license taken away for good. So far, it hasn't happened.

"How much does it cost to get into a movie these days?" he wants to know.

"I don't know what it costs where you are," I say. "It's about ten dollars here."

"I'll charge five," he says. "I bought a movie projector. We can watch movies when you come for Christmas."

I try to get excited, but this is hard for me to imagine. When I go home for Christmas, I don't see him. Never have. Never planned to. He goes into his room, closes the door, and plays his guitar. I close my door, too.

My father and I will watch movies at Christmas. My whole family— and Gurpreet, too—will watch movies together at Christmas. I say the words over and over in my head. It's hard to fathom.

I am afraid to get too excited, afraid it won't come true. If it doesn't, I'll be fine. Always have been. Always will be.

No. That is not the truth. I have not been fine at all.

"How much is popcorn at the movies?" he asks. I can tell he's enjoying this.

"It's more expensive than the movie, Dad."

"I'll get Mom to pop some popcorn and sell it to you and Gurpreet. Our popcorn will be cheap. It'll only cost you five dollars apiece. Do you think that's fair?" he asks, with laughter in his voice.

"It's highway robbery!" I exclaim, a big smile on my face. Then I get serious again.

"Dad, what would you think if I went to Vietnam next year?"

I wait for him to throw a fit and ask why in the world I'd ever want to go there. Once again, my father surprises me.

"If you want to go, go on," he says. "How much will it cost?"

"I don't know yet. There's a group of veterans and children of veterans that are planning a trip next year. I think I want to go."

"Go to Saigon," he says. "It's called Ho Chi Minh City now. That's in the South. I was only in the South. We didn't go up North."

"What did Vietnam look like, Dad?"

"I can't hardly remember. Sure can't. Just can't remember. I wasn't paying no attention to what it looked like. It's really warm. Certain months, they have monsoons. Where I was, they had monsoons around Christmas."

"What were you paying attention to?" I ask.

"The enemy. Staying alive," he says flatly.

"That old jungle grows fast," he goes on. "We used machetes to cut trails. But that stuff grows so fast, a week or two later, you can't even tell where you've been. You lose track of it all. Nothing looks the same.

"There are water buffalos there," he continues. "Like cattle, only bigger and meaner. They'll chase you, run you down. Every time one tried to run me down, I'd shoot it. We all did. Those water buffalos are what those old farmers over there plowed with."

"Would you be interested in going to Vietnam with me?"

"No," he says. "I can't go back there. Can't go back there." He pauses. "I can't afford it. I'll let you go," he says. "I can't go back over there."

"Do you have any good memories from the war?" I ask.

"No, I don't. Not a single one. Well, maybe one. I went to Saigon for in-country R&R. Saigon was the capital of South Vietnam."

"What did you do there?"

"Just walked up and down the streets. I rode the rickshaws. They pulled those things by hand."

"Did you like it?" I ask.

"It was alright. That's where I got the cane. The one with the dragon head. From Saigon."

Mom wants to talk again, so I say good-bye to my father.

"It's hard to think," she tells me. "I can't write anymore, and I have a hard time breathing at times."

"What does the doctor say?"

"He doesn't say anything anymore, just writes me more prescriptions and asks how I'm doing. Last time I was there, he asked me if I had any children and if they lived close to home."

"Why did he ask you that?"

I know why—and I don't want to think about it.

"You never know what will happen," she says. "You never know."

I do. I am so afraid I do.

"I want to ask you a question," she says. "Would it be safe for me to go to Vietnam with you?"

Her question absolutely stuns me. Just a few minutes ago she was anxious about even *my* going. She's ill and having problems with her medication, yet now she wants to know if she can go with me. No way I'll take her with me, but I can't tell her that flat-out.

My thoughts churn as I try to articulate an answer. "I have to think about it, Mom," is the only response I can come up with.

Journal

My father was sometimes fun to be around—when he was taking his medication (which I suspect he didn't always do, given the volatility of his mood swings) and when he was playing his guitar. When he was able to go to church, he'd take his guitar to the front and sing.

This was usually during the altar call, when all the sinners were given an opportunity to come to the front and "get saved."

Everyone would close their eyes and holler "Amen" as my father sang. He wrote his own songs, most of them about Jesus. At the end of church, as I walked out the door, the elders would shake my hand and tell me how lucky I was to have a father like that.

Their words left my throat dry. My response was always the same. I'd nod, smile, and wish I could tell them all the things they didn't know—about how he used to chase me through the house during one of his rages, scream at my mother and me, lock himself in his room during his bouts of depression, and periodically take his gun to the river when he became suicidal.

My mother said my father was a good person.

"It's *Vietnam*," she'd always whisper. "It's not his fault. It's *Vietnam*."

The word "Vietnam" took shape, became alive, a thing to fear. It was deep, dark, and unpredictable, a force that could take hold of a person and not let go.

"There may be no getting over the things your father has seen and done," my mother said, her voice low.

What was she trying to tell me?

Hope, but not too much? Pray, but it might not help? Have faith in his doctors, though there may be nothing they can do?

So sometimes I felt sorry for my father, and sometimes I wished he would die. And all the while I loved him and wondered if the war really had made him like he was or if it was just him.

Day Sixteen

My father wants to know what I did today. He tells me he has to go to the VA hospital tomorrow. The one in Johnson City is an hour and a half drive from his house.

"Did you get to go to the VA hospital in Atlanta to look around yet?" he asks me.

"No, not yet," I say. I've been avoiding it. My fears of seeing people with missing arms or legs have returned. I saw enough of that when I went with my dad at around the age of eight, and the whole experience gave me nightmares. Now I'm afraid I'll have those nightmares again.

"Why do you have to go to the VA tomorrow?" I ask.

"My eyes," he says.

"What's wrong with your eyes?"

"The doctors just check my glasses every year."

"How often do you go to the VA?" I ask.

"Every two or three months."

"Why do you go so often?"

"I have to go to my primary care doctor."

Going to the doctor that often isn't normal. Something must be wrong with my father. What if he is dying? What if I don't know? What if he's keeping it a secret?

"That doesn't make sense," I say. "Every two or three months? That's a lot, isn't it?"

"They keep checking on me all the time," my father says. From the sound of his voice, I can tell he's annoyed by my questioning, but I can't stop myself.

"Dad, what have you been treated for over the past few years?" There must be a running list. Some of the things I remember, but I've never asked him this question before.

"PTSD, for one, and my lung. The hernia. And I had acid reflux for a long time. I have allergies really bad now," he says.

I remember when he had the lung operation. I will never forget how he looked with all those tubes. It scared me to death to see him that way. I don't want to think about it.

"What about the cysts?" I ask, pulling myself back to the present.

"What cysts?" he wants to know.

"The cysts on your fingers. Don't you go to the VA for that, too?"

"What are you talking about?"

"The cysts on your fingers. You know. You had surgery to remove them. You just had surgery last year."

"Oh," he says. "Lord, I forgot. They've cut me open so many times, I didn't remember that. I can't remember things. They cut half my brain out in that hospital." He laughs.

"That's silly," I say. "They didn't cut your brain out. You've never had brain surgery. I'd know."

Wouldn't I?

God, *Wouldn't* I?

He laughs again. He is kidding. I think.

"Those fellers took half my brain out, Christal," he says.

It's a joke. I'm sure of it now.

"Why'd they take half your brain out, Dad?" I ask, playing along.

"They didn't need all of it. They just needed half."

"Why'd they need half?"

He cackles. He thinks he has gotten one over on me. "They didn't take no brain out, honey," he says.

I want to know more about his medical history. My entire childhood, I carried bags and bags of pills shipped from the VA from the mailbox to our trailer and helped my mother put them away. I never really knew what they were for, and I never dared ask.

"What kinds of medications does the VA have you on?" I ask.

"Stomach medication. High-cholesterol medication. Two blood-pressure medications. Allergy pills. Posttraumatic stress medicine," he says.

God, so much medication. I didn't know. No one told me he had high blood pressure. No one told me he had high cholesterol. Did they?

I can't remember.

"What do they have you on for PTSD?"

"I don't know what the name of that stuff is. It's just medication. They change it every now and then."

"Why do they change it?"

"They just change it," he says. "They change it when they get a better deal on another medication."

"Are you on antidepressants?"

"One of them is an antidepressant, probably. One of the PTSD medications."

"Did you know I used to take antidepressants, Dad?"

He is concerned now. His voice changes. "What kind did you take? Do you still take them?"

I don't tell him what kind. There were so many. I don't want to freak him out and send him into an episode. "I'm not on them anymore," I say, immediately sorry that I brought it up. I'd taken antidepressants on and off since college to help regulate my emotions, but I hadn't taken them in three years because they made me either bounce off the walls or sleep all the time. I stopped taking them when I realized I could handle the depression better than I could deal with the side effects of the drugs.

His whole demeanor has changed, and he doesn't want to talk about this anymore. Neither do I. It's time to move on.

"Avery's up here in my lap," he says. "He comes upstairs every night. He won't go to bed until I do."

"Duma is the same way," I say of my little dog. "He won't go to bed unless I go to bed, too." Duma is with me now, his little body curled into a ball beside me, his head resting against my leg.

"Did you go to church today and play your guitar, Dad?" I ask.

"Yes. Went to Clintwood."

"Did you play your song about the war?"

"No. Not today."

"What's your favorite song you've ever written?"

He pauses and thinks.

"I don't know. I don't like none of them," he says.

I don't believe him.

"Why don't you like any song you've written?" I ask. "That doesn't make sense."

"I just don't like them. It doesn't matter about me. It's other people that have to like them or not like them. I just write them down."

I never knew he felt that way. Funny thing is, I feel that way, too. I can love what I write, but unless other people like it, I don't feel fulfilled. It seems to me that my father and I both need validation from others to feel validated ourselves.

Seems like this is yet another thing we have in common. This realization makes me feel even more connected to him.

"Do *you* like my songs?" His voice is kind, gentle. He wants to know what I think. It matters.

"Yes," I say.

"A little or a lot?"

"A lot."

"Would you pay to hear me sing?" he asks.

"I would," I say. I mean it. "Dad?" I ask quietly.

"What, Christal? What's wrong?"

"Why do you want me to go to the VA hospital?"

"I want you to see the soldiers, I guess," he says. "Their legs are blown off, their arms blown off, they're not right in the head. But you don't have to go. You don't have to see that. Maybe you don't want to go."

"No," I say. "I do." He's just confirmed exactly what I was afraid of. But, much as I dread it, I feel that I have to go. I don't know why, but I do.

"Mommy's going with me to the VA tomorrow," he says.

"What does she do there?" I ask. I think about all the times I went, when I stayed in the car, curled into a little ball on top of the floor mats, hiding from what I thought were crazy people.

"She walks around and looks for other men," he says. "She wants to get her another husband. What do you think about that?" He laughs.

It is not funny to me.

"No, she doesn't," I say. "That is ridiculous."

"She could at least wait until I'm dead, couldn't she?" He stops. "Well, I guess I'm already dead." He is more serious now.

"Stop it," I say. "Don't say that. Why would you say that?"

"I just said it to be saying it."

Did he *really*? I am not convinced.

"Do you ever try to sing?" he asks.

"No. I can't sing." I haven't sung in years.

"But you used to sing with me."

"I know," I say. "But I can't sing like you. I don't like to sing anymore."

"Reckon they'll make a movie about my life?" he wants to know. "I may be more famous than Elvis. Reckon? Mommy says I'm not no Elvis, though. That feller Elvis could sing. . . . I love you, Christal," he says at the end.

"I love you, too, Dad." I say quietly. This conversation with my father has put me in a pensive mood. There's still so much I don't know about him, and there's so much he doesn't know about me. I don't know if it's possible to make up for the thirteen years we barely spoke, but it is some consolation to know that the more I talk to him, the more I realize how much we are alike. And at the very same time, in some ways, it's unsettling.

Journal

In sixth grade I bought candy cigarettes and held them to my mouth when I was sure someone was looking. Maybe a coach, a neighbor, or a teacher. Someone who would ask what I thought I was doing. No one ever did. I dotted my body with a red magic marker and told everyone they were blisters. Of course, no one believed me, but again, no one asked why I'd done that.

I scratched my babysitter's new car with a rock, digging Xs into the maroon paint below the keyhole. No one suspected me. With red fingernail polish, I painted my name on the back of the school bus seat. The next day the bus driver handed me a bottle of polish remover and told me to clean it. He never told anyone else. I took a sharp nail file and gutted another bus seat, picking the foam out of the inside in hunks. That time I was called into the assistant principal's office. He scolded me but didn't ask why I had done it; nor did he call my parents. I was a straight-A student, and as far as he knew I'd never done anything like that before, so he let me off easy.

"If you could be any color, what would you be?" my sixth-grade English teacher asked one day.

I could not decide. There were too many choices.

"Blue," said one boy.

"Purple," said a girl named Lynessa who had just moved from Florida.

"Orange."

"Pink."

"Green."

"Clear," I said finally, when the teacher insisted I participate. "I am invisible. I do not have a color."

The classroom became so silent that you could have heard a pin drop. Everyone including the teacher stared at me as I stared at the floor, mortified. I'd finally gotten their attention, and I didn't know what to do except cower in shame.

The teacher, clearly taken aback and trying to remedy an awkward situation, quickly moved on to ask the next student what color she'd like to be.

Before eighth grade, I was in the Gifted and Talented program, participated in school plays, won the talent show two years in a row, and kept my grades up. I won awards for writing, was on the academic team, and was voted most valuable player on my softball team. In truth, this gave me plenty of opportunities to make friends and interact with people. But because I was constantly torn between the desperate need to tell my family secret and the fear of what would happen if I did, I never let anyone get too close.

Because I was doing well, and because I kept people at arm's length, everyone more or less ignored my oddness—at least until middle school. But that didn't last.

There was a girl in my seventh-grade homeroom named Jodi. I usually sat with her at lunch, and sometimes I spent the night at her house.

Jodi lived in a brand-new brick house at the foot of House and Barn Mountain, which had two massive rock formations at the top, one bigger than the other. People said the little one was a house, the bigger one a barn. That's how the mountain got its name. If you saw the mountain from a distance and used a lot of imagination, you could see it.

Jodi and I lay on her bed some Friday nights and listened to her collection of CDs. She had hundreds—from Crash Test Dummies to Paula Abdul to New Kids on the Block. Janet Jackson was my favorite. Jodi and I turned off all the lights and danced to the music in the dark. It didn't seem like dancing then. No one could see me. It couldn't really be a sin if no one was watching.

We talked about what brands of pads we used when we had our periods and what astringents worked best on our pimples. Jodi used tampons, which fascinated me. My mother had said it was best that a woman didn't use tampons until she was married, but she didn't say why.

"That's crazy," Jodi said. "I've never heard of that."

I shrugged my shoulders. "It's what she said."

We leafed through her mother's romance books, turned down the corners of the pages where there were sex scenes. We read the pages silently with our music in the background, poked each other and giggled, traded books and pointed to particularly poignant passages.

"Do you think Ms. Crause has sex?" I asked Jodi about our science teacher.

"She's married, isn't she?" she said.

"Still," I said. "I wonder if she has sex."

We let another song play, this one by Milli Vanilli.

"Do you think your parents have sex?" I whispered.

She frowned. "Gross," she said. "I don't want to think about it."

"They probably don't," I said. "When you're old, I don't think you have sex anymore."

She nodded. "You're probably right."

I did not tell her about my father locked up in his room or anything else. When I was at Jodi's house, I could pretend to be normal. I didn't invite her to my house where there was no telling what my father would do.

When we decided to do our science fair project together, her parents could not take us to the local library. My mother was working so she couldn't take us either. We'd waited until the last minute, and now we were stuck. I squirmed when my father offered to take us. Maybe he could do it this once. Maybe everything would be okay.

"We can't stay long," I said to Jodi, after he'd dropped us off. He was waiting outside, and I knew how impatient he could be. "We need to go in, get what we need, and get out."

She nodded, clearly confused at the rush.

"You find three books, and I'll get three," I told her. "We meet back here in ten minutes."

I breathed a sigh of relief when Jodi came back on time with her three books. This was going to be simple. Everything was going to be okay.

I had my library card, but Jodi had forgotten hers. My plan was to check out all the books in my name. But when the librarian scanned my card she saw that I had an outstanding fine. "I can't let you check out anything until you pay the fine," she said.

My heart fell. I looked at Jodi. I had forgotten about that fine. I'd left a book outside in the rain when I was playing with my dogs. The fine was for its replacement cost.

"Do you have five dollars?" I asked Jodi. *Please, God, let her say yes.*

She shook her head and looked at me solemnly. "I didn't bring any money."

I would have to ask my father. It was either that or get a zero on the science project, and back then, I still cared about my grades.

I asked Jodi to stay put. I would go back to the car to talk to my father alone.

What happened after that was worse than anything I'd imagined.

When I asked for the money and admitted what had happened to the book, he flew into a rage. He got out of the car, stomped and swore, slammed the door so hard the car shook. His anger gauge was through the roof. He took off into the library like a violent storm, with me trailing behind him.

What was he going to do? God, what would he do in there? I knew he'd be mad, but it wasn't like him to act like this in public. He'd gotten as good at pretending as my mother and me.

"She is not to check out any books!" he yelled at the librarian as soon as he walked through the door.

Twenty feet away, she sat quietly at her desk near the counter. He shook the whole place with his voice as people looked up in astonishment. Everyone was watching.

There was a look of panic on the librarian's face. Should she call someone? Was it safe to move? What was happening?

Just a few feet away, Jodi held her three books. Her mouth was open and her face went white. She did not move. I wanted to crawl into a hole and die.

In the end, my father shoved the money for the fine across the counter, and I checked out my books without saying a word, my eyes fixed on the floor. I could not even fathom looking at the librarian because I was so humiliated, and I didn't want her to see my tears.

As soon as we were back in the car I broke out in sobs. Neither my father nor Jodi said a word. He was still furious, and she was in a total state of shock.

When we got to Jodi's house to drop her off, I pulled myself together enough to walk her to her door. Her face was gray by then.

"I don't think you'd better come in today," she said, looking down at the ground.

I nodded, sniffling and wiping my eyes. I was afraid that if I tried to talk I'd just start sobbing all over again.

Jodi never asked me to come to her house again, and from that point on, she avoided me as much as possible.

Day Seventeen

I call my father on the way to therapy because I'm thinking about him and I want to hear his voice.

"Where are you going?" he asks when I tell him that I'm driving.

I want to lie. "I'm going to therapy," I say reluctantly.

I can't remember if he knows I've ever been to therapy. If he knows, he's never mentioned it.

He is quiet, gentle. "How long have you been in therapy?" he asks in a soft voice.

God, I wasn't expecting that. Let me think of a big one, something to throw him off the subject, something to make him forget he ever asked. "Years," I say instead. "I've been in therapy on and off for years."

I feel relieved to finally admit this to him. I also hold my breath and hope I haven't just triggered another bout of depression.

His voice is even and composed when he speaks. "What is your diagnosis?" he asks.

It shocks me that he would even think to ask this question, and I pause, wondering whether I should even respond. "I have PTSD."

"Who told you that?" he asks, his voice still steady.

"A therapist when I was in college," I say, biting my bottom lip as I wait for him to tell me that it's impossible because I never went to war; *he* did.

But my father does not respond as I expected him to. In fact, he doesn't respond at all. Instead there's a long silence as I imagine him trying to wrap his mind around what I've just told him.

"Well, call me back tonight for sure," he says finally. "I hope your therapy appointment goes well. . . . And decide when you're coming in for Christmas, okay? You *are* still coming, aren't you?"

I take a deep breath and exhale slowly. Telling the truth about myself to my father has been more liberating than I would have expected.

"Of course I'm coming home," I say confidently. Especially now.

● ● ●

"Why do you want to go to Vietnam?" my therapist asks.

She leans back in her chair and crosses her legs. She is thinking hard. I can tell she approves of this trip. But she wants to know why. She wants *me* to know why.

I don't know. It's hard to explain.

"I need to see," I tell her.

"See what?" she wants to know.

"I need to see where my father went."

"Why do you need to see?"

I close my eyes and rub my hands over my face.

"I guess I want to see that they've moved on," I say. "That the Vietnamese have moved on from the war. In the pictures I've seen of what it's like today it looks so peaceful."

"Will it help *you* move on?" she asks.

I shrug my shoulders. "I don't know. I think so. I want to see where my father was back then. Back before I was born."

"Will it help you understand him?" she asks.

"I think so." Lord, I don't know anything these days.

"Why is it you think you can take a trip to Vietnam, but it's uncomfortable to go to the VA hospital a few miles from here?" she asks.

I shift in my seat as I cross my arms.

"I'm *going* to the VA hospital," I tell her. "I just haven't yet."

"Why are you uncomfortable with it, Christal?"

"I have awful memories of the VA hospital from when I was a child. I don't look forward to seeing mangled people or people who are out of their minds."

"Why?" she probes further.

My head hurts.

"What is it about those veterans you don't want to see?" she persists.

I don't know. I don't know. I don't know. I don't know.

"They cannot get away from the war," I finally say.

Like my father.

• • •

It's later than usual when I call him that evening. My mother answers the phone.

"I don't want you to be mad," I tell her, "but I think it's best that you don't go to Vietnam with me." I've known all along that I couldn't take her, but this is the first time I've said it to her. I hope she doesn't want to know why. I don't want to remind her of how sick she is, and I don't want her to know that she'd just be a burden.

Thankfully, she doesn't ask me to explain. I can tell she's disappointed, but I'm not convinced she would have come anyway. "I understand," is all that she says.

"What's wrong?" my father asks when she gives the phone to him.

"I'm exhausted," I say. "And nervous. My defense for that big paper I've been working on is this Friday."

"Are you ready?" he wants to know, his voice encouraging.

I'm not sure. My mind is still on Vietnam.

"Do you want me to go to Vietnam?" I ask my father. I want to hear what he has to say.

"If you want to," he says.

"But I'm asking you if *you* want me to, Dad."

"Whatever," he says. "If you want to."

I want him to say yes. I want him to *want* me to go. Partly I guess I'm still trying to get his approval and partly I need him to say that he wants me to see where he was. If he wants me to go I'll feel that my decision is validated.

"You are difficult," I say. I plop down in my chair, close my eyes.

"So are you," he says.

Journal

The preacher at our little church said you'd always remember the day you got saved. Getting saved was when you asked Jesus Christ to be your personal savior, when you asked Him to forgive your sins.

You could not officially get saved until you were twelve. Our church deemed that the "age of accountability," the age at which you had the sense to know what you were doing and make the decision for yourself.

You could get saved at any time during church service. You'd simply walk up to the altar, fall upon your knees, cry, and make a commotion as you admitted to Jesus what a horrible person you were. Most people would wait until after the altar call, which came at the end of the preacher's message.

Preacher Ray would stand in the pulpit with holy water, sobbing as he begged anyone who "didn't have Christ in his heart" to come get saved.

He called my name into a microphone right after my twelfth birthday and said I looked like Jesus had put me under conviction. I was so panic-stricken that my first reaction was to crawl under my pew and hide. Now everyone in the church would know that I was a horrible person.

I couldn't bear to have them look at me afterward. I couldn't stand seeing the disapproval in their eyes. So I pulled myself together and went to the altar to pray because I was afraid not to. Preacher Ray had called my name, singled me out. I knew what was expected of me.

Soon as I got up, my mother followed, and my Mamaw Short-ridge, too. They knelt at the altar with me, and we prayed together.

Please, Jesus, save me from my sins. Make my daddy okay, I prayed over and over.

I felt nothing.

When enough time had passed for me to have gotten saved, I stood up and looked at the congregation. My mother and grand-mother stood up, too.

Preacher Ray pushed the microphone into my face. As was tradition, it was time for me to testify. I looked to my mother. She nodded.

I knew what to do.

"I thank Jesus for saving me," I said. "And I thank Him for having such a happy family."

I smiled.

By twelve, I had perfected the art of acting. To everyone else, my smile and my words were as sincere as they came. No one could see my clenched teeth.

I always wondered if people in the church suspected anything was wrong with my father. Sometimes he was friendly; other times he was cold and distant. His eyes could go from peaceful to sheer frenzy in an instant. Mostly, however, he had a knack for pretending when he was around other people. We all did.

In my imagination, a thousand times, I voiced a different testimony to the congregation than the one I gave that day.

You don't know what it's like. You don't know the way we live, I envisioned myself saying.

In my mind, I told them about the pads my father slept on at night to catch the sweat from his nightmares, his cabinets full of pills, the way he locked himself in his room away from his family, the times he threatened to blow his brains out when he took his gun to the river.

I knew all the while I didn't get saved.

The only thing that could save me was leaving that place for good.

Day Eighteen

Before I call my dad tonight, I look through the pictures in the albums my mother left with me. I've been doing that a lot lately, and I see a smiling little girl in every one of them.

This little girl likes bright colors and patterns. She has a blue snowsuit and a pink and purple ten-speed bike. She tears through the yard in her socks. She's an eight-year-old in a fake fur coat. She sprawls out on top of her father's brown Nova to sun herself.

"Who are you?" I ask the girl in the pictures.

She stares back at me and smiles.

"I know you have secrets," I tell her. "No one will ask you. You will not tell them. Not for a very long time."

In one picture she looks over her shoulder while playing the piano. She doesn't even have to look at the notes. She wears clothes her mother sewed herself, stands on her head until all the blood rushes to her brain, and presses pinecones between her hands.

She looks right at me, this girl in the pictures. She laughs.

142

I want to scoop her up and take her to a place where she doesn't have to hide. A safe place. One where she can keep her good memories.

The girl in the pictures does not pay me much mind. She pushes her orange cat named Tiger in a stroller, turns flips on her trampoline, and buries herself in piles of leaves. She walks through the woods like her father. Goes to the river like her father.

"Look at me," I say to her. "I have something to tell you. It will be okay. No matter what happens, it will be okay. I need you to know this," I tell her.

She gets up from that Nova, stretches her legs, pops the top on her thermos, and takes a swig.

She looks through the picture and nods back at me.

"No, I need *you* to know it," she says.

• • •

"*Doctor* Presley?" my dad asks tentatively. He doesn't know how the defense went. He's feeling me out. Did I pass or did I fail?

"Yeah," I say. I am.

God, I am.

"Doctor Presley." It's not a question this time. "Boy, that sounds good." He's smiling. I know it. "Now I can tell everyone that my girl's a doctor. It all goes back to me. Ain't you glad you got a smart father?"

He cracks me up. I don't know what to say to something like that.

"I am, Dad."

"I got a head on my shoulders," he says. "Ain't got nothing between my ears, but I got a head on my shoulders." He goes on, "Instead of giving you twenty-five dollars for Christmas, I'll give you fifty, okay?" He doesn't wait for me to answer. "When do you get your raise?"

I laugh. "I don't know."

"I'm proud of you. I really am," he repeats. "My girl is a doctor." He can't say it enough.

Truth to tell, I'm exhausted from the stress of defending my dissertation, and I'm delighted that he doesn't want to talk about the war tonight. It's just nice to hear his praise.

Life is a funny thing.

The violets in the mountains have broken the rocks.

Journal

When I reached high school, I was so depressed that I couldn't focus on academics. Ten years of emotional turmoil had finally taken its toll. In class I participated when I was in the mood. Otherwise, I just sat there and stared into space. My grades plummeted. I didn't care.

I no longer viewed each passing birthday as a mile marker toward maturity. By then, I was in countdown mode. Each birthday came to mean that I was another year closer to leaving my family, leaving my life behind, and starting over. Another year closer to getting away from the war.

I had thoughts of running my car into a tree. It was an accident. That's what I'd say. I hit some gravel on the side of the road and lost control. Maybe people would notice me then.

Before I got my first boyfriend, I promised older boys I'd have sex with them on the first date if only they'd go out with me. I never had to make good on that promise, though—because they never went out with me. I fantasized about having affairs with teachers and neighbors. I longed to be touched, to be held by a man.

I sat on the bench during basketball games.

"What happened to Christal?" people asked. "She was in the starting lineup last year."

"She's not trying very hard," the teachers said. "Must be her boyfriend. This is her first boyfriend, and she's distracted." I heard them in the teachers' lounge one day when I was passing by. It was a logical assumption. I had just begun going out with the boy I would date for the next four years. What no one knew—and what I was never able to articulate back then—was that I was so depressed, I'd lost the motivation to do much of anything. Giving up basketball had nothing at all to do with my boyfriend.

"What do you want to be?" Ms. Smith, the guidance counselor, asked one day during my junior year. She stuffed a pile of SAT prep booklets in my hands. Their cheap ink rubbed off on my T-shirt.

I didn't know what I wanted to be. I was not in college mode. I was just trying to survive.

I had to leave, had to get out of that place. But *could* I? *Would* I?

Hardly anyone I knew left those mountains of Virginia. Plus, I didn't have any money for college.

I shrugged my shoulders. The world was heavy. "I guess I'll be a bus driver or a cosmetologist," I told Ms. Smith.

She nodded, wrote a few things in her notebook, and sent me back to class.

By senior year, the only sport I played was softball. I went to practice when I felt like it, but I preferred volunteering at the veterinary clinic. The animals did not judge me. They sat and listened. They were the only ones I could tell that I hoped I died young if this was what it felt like to live.

Even though I was desperate for people to notice me, it was agonizing to be around other people. They talked too much, laughed too much, never watched their backs.

My softball teammates paced the dugout, spit sunflower seeds all over the sandy floor, threw their gloves down on the bench, and clinked bats against the concrete walls. There was too much activity. Too much. Too much. Why couldn't they be still?

They whooped and hollered, cheered our teammates on while I sat silent. The noise was too loud. It hurt my ears. Why couldn't they stop screaming?

My father came to my games when he felt up to it. My mother came when she didn't have to work. My father was on disability by then. My mother had gone to nursing school, had gotten her degree, and had become a nurse. Except for my father's disability checks, she was the sole support of our family. I was proud of my mother and at the same time resentful, because her nursing schedule meant she often had to work evenings and weekends, which meant that I was left alone in the house with my father.

It was after my mom became a nurse that I began to develop lesions on my skin. I picked my scalp until it bled, then started on the insides of my ears. I wouldn't find out until years later that what I had was psoriasis, and that its symptoms can be aggravated by stress.

"She has no school spirit," everyone said. "What is going on?"

They never asked me. I did not tell.

Day Nineteen

I wake up this morning and decide that I will go to the VA hospital today.

I feel ready. The time has come.

My neighbor Mary has said that she would go with me if I wanted.

Lord, it's hard for me to ask. It's dangerous to get close to people, to let them in.

But I want to. I know I *need* to.

Mary is a good person. She's kind and open-minded, an artist and an actress. She's been on Broadway. She lives with her partner, Elizabeth, a few doors down the street. Elizabeth is a good person, too. She was an actress like Mary, but she got fed up with doing commercials and now she does pharmaceutical research.

They are exactly the kind of people you should welcome into your life, my psyche tells me.

Why is it so hard? Why is it so comfortable to be alone?

It's easy for me to form relationships with the teachers I mentor and with their students. Why is talking to my own neighbors so hard? Our houses are tightly packed in this part of Atlanta. I have hundreds of neighbors, always smiling and waving. I walk past their houses quickly, hope they won't see me, or avoid walking past them altogether.

I text Mary, and she says she can go.

"How do you feel?" Mary asks me several times along the way.

I feel okay, not weepy or falling to pieces like I thought I would. I feel strong. Ready.

This is an important part of getting to know my father, and I am proud to do it.

The VA hospital is neither beautiful nor ugly. It's a plain-looking high-rise in cream, yellow, and blue, with several other buildings attached. It is clean, well-maintained, under construction.

Under construction. That's my favorite part. There is still life here.

We walk through the first floor, and pass a smiling man in a Vietnam veterans' cap. My heart skips a beat. I wish I'd stopped him. There was such a brightness in his eyes.

Everyone we pass is smiling. This is not like the VA hospital I remember.

A man with no legs wheels by and nods. To my amazement he's smiling and his eyes look bright. There is a large plastic bag in his lap, with Christmas trinkets sticking out the top. He's been shopping at the hospital shop.

I can do this. I know I can do this.

Mary and I enter the shop and rummage through a box of hats. Someone has come up behind us.

I look up and see the man from before. The one with the bright eyes and a Vietnam veterans' cap. This time I don't let him get away.

"Were you in Vietnam?" I ask.

He smiles. "Signed up for the air force and went there," he says. "In 1965."

"My father was in Vietnam, too," I say.

This is our code. We are one.

He tells us that his name is Frank, that he's sixty-six, that he processed bodies in the war. "That means I matched the bodies with the families," he says. "Processed twenty-one hundred of them."

His face changes, his eyes are distant. I know that look. I see my father in him.

"You never get over something like that," he says. "You never get over it."

Frank has six children and hasn't spoken to the first three in twenty-three years. The other three he texts once a week, talks to once a month. He goes to group meetings at the VA once a week, says they help more than anything else.

"We don't talk about the past," he says. "I couldn't deal with that. We talk about what's happening right now, and we help each other get through that."

He wants to know if my father likes to be alone.

"He does," I say. "So do I. I could go months without seeing anyone and be fine."

"You got that from your father," he says. "I'm like that, too."

I tell Frank that my father has posttraumatic stress disorder and that I have symptoms as well.

Frank has PTSD, too. "I didn't know what it was until the nineties," he says. "Before that, I just thought I was crazy. I didn't know what was wrong with me, but I knew something was." He pauses for a moment. "Do you think your symptoms of PTSD came from your father's symptoms?"

I nod.

I wonder how Frank's symptoms affected his children. If so, it wasn't his fault. He couldn't help it. I'd finally accepted that about my own dad. I wondered if they knew it, too.

"Does your father go to funerals?" Frank wants to know. "I haven't been to a funeral since nineteen sixty-seven. Can't stand it anymore. Can't stand to look at dead people."

"He does go to funerals," I say. "But funerals are such social events where I come from. He goes to funerals to play his guitar. Everyone always asks him to play."

It is I who have always been scared to death of funerals. Our town only had one funeral home, and my mother and I were there every week. When no one was looking, I'd hide in a broom closet.

"I'm buying a cap for my father," I say to Frank. "And a matching one for myself." I hold up two black caps that read VIETNAM VETERAN. They look a lot like the one he is wearing.

"My father loves things that say VIETNAM VETERAN," I say. "He has belt buckles, jackets, caps. He doesn't have a cap like this, though."

"We find each other when we wear those things," Frank says. "I do it, too. It's the only way for us to see each other sometimes. If we didn't wear them, we'd look like regular people."

It's making more sense now. I don't know why I didn't think of this before.

"Your father plays the guitar all the time, huh?" he says. "Well, I don't have a guitar, but I have a laptop. I watch movies the way your dad plays the guitar. I always have my laptop on me, always have a movie ready."

I understand.

I always have a notepad with me. It is my guitar. My laptop. My medicine.

"You all are easy for me to talk to," Frank says. "It's because I know I'll never see you again. I can't get close to people. I just can't do it," he explains. "Not anymore."

For a moment, I am looking at myself. At my father. At my whole life in this man who is a stranger but whom I know so well.

"Your face is so bright. So alive," Mary tells him.

He laughs. "Maybe that's the Spanish in me," he says.

"I'm glad I met you, Frank," I say. "Thank you for serving our country."

"Thank you so much for saying that," he says.

Mary and I agree that even if we left right now, the whole day would be worth it. But we forge on.

The hospital is quiet; all of the office doors are closed. We do not venture onto the floors where there are patients. We'll save this for another day.

We end up in the nursing-home section before we leave. This is where the soldiers who live here stay. I don't know what I'll see, but I am not afraid anymore.

We pass men in wheelchairs, one with a little fur hat. He has thick glasses and looks like an elf. Mary and I exchange smiles. We see bald men watching TV and playing board games. Every room is bright, colorful, and decorated for Christmas. Everyone acknowledges us and waves. This is not like I thought it would be.

On our way out, we pass a man in a rocking chair. His skin is the color of coffee, smooth like silk. He wears sweatpants and a sweatshirt with a colorful knit cap on his head. He rocks back and forth, back and forth.

"Are you all touring?" he asks.

"Sort of," I say. "Do we look lost?"

"No," he says. "You don't look lost."

"What war were you in?" I ask.

"Vietnam," he says.

Stopping here is no mistake.

Harvey is hard to understand, talks a mile a minute, rocks back and forth all the while. Mary looks away, props herself up against the wall. He is making her dizzy.

We can only pick up bits and pieces of what he says. He tells us that his thumb hurts, but the nurses put him in a wheelchair like he is supposed to wheel himself around. This doesn't make sense, he thinks. Harvey is funny. A lot of other things don't make sense to him either. The telephones are bugged, he says. So are the wheelchairs and the TVs. He would have been a millionaire by now, but Motown stole all the songs he wrote, gave them to other artists to record.

"That is what happens when the Mafia is after you," he says. "And the government, too."

Harvey has two kids who are still alive. One has been in jail. It's hard to pick up anything else.

"Thank you for talking to Mr. Harvey," says one of the nurses as she walks by. "Mr. Harvey likes to talk, but no one comes to talk to him. He mostly talks to us," she says.

"Thank you for serving your country," I tell Harvey. He nods his head, rocks back and forth.

"Thank you, thank you, thank you," he says, in time with his chair.

He is still waving as we turn the corner.

• • •

"Has your head gone down?" my dad wants to know. I assume he means that I must be very proud of having successfully defended my dissertation. In fact, he's not wrong about that.

"Yes," I say.

"Mine hasn't," he says proudly. "I told them in church this morning that I had to sleep on the sofa last night because my head was swelled so big I couldn't get through my bedroom door." He pauses. "I am proud of you," he adds. "I think I'm even prouder of you than Mommy is."

"So what do I get?" I say.

He laughs. "What do you want? I said I'd give you fifty dollars for Christmas. That's double what I usually do."

I laugh.

"When are you coming?" he wants to know.

"Probably the twenty-third. I don't get off until then."

"I'll take you out to eat that night, okay?"

"Okay, Dad."

"What did you do today?" he asks.

I smile. "I went to the VA hospital."

"Tell me about that," he says, clearly excited.

I cannot wait.

Journal

Donavan Bridges was my first boyfriend. I met him when I was fifteen, a sophomore in high school. I had PE at the end of the day, and was walking out of the school gym just as he was walking in to visit with an old coach of his. Out of nowhere he struck up a conversation with me and asked for my phone number. He was twenty, a junior in college. Thus began my obsession with older men.

My parents liked him immediately because I assured them he was a Christian. The fact that he was five years older than me didn't seem to matter to them. And, in any case, he was a charmer—tall and good-looking with dark hair and eyes.

When he pulled into the driveway on our first date, my mother just happened to be getting home from the grocery store where she'd stopped after work. He unloaded all the groceries from her car and wouldn't let her carry a single bag into the house. After that, Donavan could do no wrong in her eyes.

Naturally, as soon as something good happened in my life, I was waiting for it to go bad. I jumped to conclusions every time Donavan was the least bit late to pick me up. More than ten minutes meant he'd probably been in an accident. I fretted that he'd run his car into a telephone pole and been thrown through the windshield. I prayed that he didn't have brain damage, that his nose was not ripped off his face like in an accident my mother described over and over that had happened to a senior at her high school.

Practically every weekend for two years, Donavan and I cruised back and forth through town in his Subaru Brat, windows rolled down, Warren G. and Snoop Dog's "Regulator" blasting through the speakers. He dreamed of buying a Nissan 300Z with T-tops. It would have a CD—not a cassette—player, so he could play his *Miami Vice* soundtrack.

"Stop picking your head," Donavan would tell me. "It's disgusting. You're getting stuff all over the car seat."

I'd recline my seat and lie down with my back against him. By this time, the psoriasis on my scalp and ears had turned into running sores.

I fantasized about marrying Donavan as soon as I graduated high school. We'd get engaged before that. Everyone was getting engaged in high school those days.

With Donavan, I felt complete. I had a chance of living happily ever after. He would be my way out of my parents' house.

Donavan was the first man I was ever physical with. I could hardly wait for us to get through our date, to get back to my house, for my parents to go to bed so that we'd be left alone. Nothing had ever felt as good as having a man hold me.

It was all I needed. *He* was all I needed.

But there were two things that bothered me. One was Donavan's family cookouts.

Every weekend, the whole Bridges clan would get together— twenty or more adults and just as many rambunctious, screaming children—to cook hamburgers and hotdogs and toast marshmal-lows. They had a fire pit with benches all around it in a little clearing in the woods behind their house.

They really talked to one another, and they expected me to partic-ipate. They asked annoying things like how was my day, what I was going to do with my life, and which subjects I liked best in school. *What did you think of the high school football game last week?* they wanted to know. *What do you think our chances are this week?*

Now I know they were being polite and trying to make me feel welcome, but at the time I felt smothered, uncomfortable. Their questions were insignificant. I didn't think they really wanted to know about me, and I could not stand to hear them speak.

Donavan's younger cousins ran circles around the pool, had sword fights with sticks, and made shooting noises with their water guns. I sat up straight, kept my eyes on them at all times, and watched my perimeter. My nerves were frazzled.

The other thing that weighed heavily on my mind was Donavan's mother.

When I had dinner at their house one evening she eyed me across the table and questioned me about my father. I don't know what she'd heard.

"You don't talk much to your dad, do you?" she said.

It wasn't the first time she'd asked.

I sat with my legs crossed and shrugged my shoulders.

"No." I tried to sound nonchalant, like it wasn't a big deal, like girls my age got asked that question all the time.

"You need to fix that," she said. "Girls who don't talk to their fathers can get into a lot of trouble later."

I squirmed. What was she trying to say? Instead of sounding sympathetic, she sounded as if she were judging me.

I didn't *need* my father. I had her son, and whether she liked it or not, I was going to marry him and live happily ever after—in another place far away from there, thank you very much.

It turned out that Donavan had plans of his own. As soon as he graduated college, he joined the navy. He could go in as an officer with a college degree. He told me that evening, after he'd signed all the paperwork and committed to serve our country for the next four years.

He wanted me to go with him. He explained that he'd be gone a few months for basic training, then I could come to wherever he was stationed. He'd marry me. We'd live happily ever after, have kids, and he would even change their diapers. What did I say?

The decision should have been an easy one—it would get me away, and that's what I wanted.

But around that time, my own life had also taken a turn. I found out that if I could get into college I could go for free because my father was a disabled veteran. It was a way out of Honaker and out of my house, and I was more excited about leaving than I was about the opportunity to receive a free education. At the time, I didn't even think about how ironic it was that the very thing I was trying to run away from—my father's PTSD—was the reason I could go to college. The government would pay my tuition for forty-eight months—four full years—and give me a monthly stipend to cover room and board . . . if I could get in.

Though I was no longer in the top tier of my class, I managed to get decent scores on my SATs. In the end, I was accepted to Virginia Tech in Blacksburg, Virginia. In order to make the most of the government's generosity, I completed both a bachelor's and a master's degree in those four years, which also gave me a great excuse to avoid going home in the summers.

Donavan's offer was still open, but I couldn't bring myself to go with him. I couldn't take the chance that he would come back like my father. Our happiness would not last—not if he went to war. I was sure of it.

I didn't care how good it felt for him to hold me, how safe or complete I felt when I was in his arms. His decision to join the military changed everything for me.

"I can't be with you anymore," I told him. It didn't matter to me that he didn't understand. I couldn't tell him my reason, only that my decision was final.

He called for months after that and left dozens of messages that said he just wanted to hear my voice.

I never picked up or called him back. I never spoke to him again.

If Donavan went to war and came back with PTSD—and I was convinced he would—I wouldn't be able to cope. In my life up to this point, fear had always trumped love.

Day Twenty

"John Fisher, the doctor who's organizing the trip to Vietnam, called tonight," I tell my father. I'm absolutely brimming with excitement. "He's designing the trip around the participants. He wants to know where you were when you were in Vietnam, Dad. I'll get to go to some of those places."

"I went to Chu Lai," my father says, sounding almost as excited as I am. "That's where my main headquarters were. Near LZ Bayonet. LZ stands for landing zone. There was another fire base called Fat City. I remember that. They were close to a road called Route 1."

"A fire base? What's that?" I ask.

"Where they store guns," he explains. "Where all the artillery is. I remember going to other landing zones, too. There was LZ Professional, LZ Gator, and I believe another was LZ Mary Ann. There was one more, too. I just can't remember the name of it. We pulled guard while they were building it. We were the first ones that went into that one. First thing we did was build a perimeter."

"Why was one called Fat City?" I ask.

"I guess the people in there were fat," he says with a chuckle.

"When you came back from war, what would you have *liked* to happen, Dad?"

I am remembering the story he'd told me about the protesters with their horrible signs and how they spit in the soldiers' faces. I want to know what would have made a positive difference for my father.

"I would've liked it if every person I met would have given me a hundred-dollar bill," he says. "That would've been good." My father is in a playful mood tonight.

For once I don't have to worry about his spiraling into a depression. Not for the moment.

"I figured people would thank me," he says, his voice becoming more serious now. "They didn't. They hated us, called us baby killers. They called us crazy. I wouldn't tell anyone I'd been in service back then. We all withdrew, went off by ourselves. Back then, if you walked downtown, the women that had children—if you had on a uniform—they would walk across the street so they wouldn't have to pass you. 'That's one of those crazy soldiers,' they'd say. They had their children thinking that way, too."

He has never told me about the women and the children before. Meeting my mother must have been a godsend for him. He was just back from the war when he saw her sitting quietly in a pew in a little country church. She was such a sweet spirit, he had said, same as she is now, didn't know a thing about the war. She was seventeen years old.

"Even when I first went down to Johnson City to the VA hospital," he says, "they didn't want to treat the Vietnam veterans. They would wait on everyone else and not wait on people like me that fought in Vietnam. They'd call everyone else and leave us sitting."

My God. I didn't know that. I'd never heard of anything like that. Is it really true? I make a mental note to do some research.

"Senator James Quillen sat down and talked to me two or three times in the VA hospital. He asked me how they were treating me. I told him how it was. He said, 'That will change.' It did after that," my father says. "They ended up naming that hospital in Johnson City after him. It's called the James H. Quillen VA Hospital now. He was a big politician, Christal. But he'd come and sit right down next to you. I liked that."

"What do you think we can do now so no more veterans will have to go through the same thing you did?" I ask my father.

"It's different now," he says. "At least, I hear tell it is. They *welcome* the troops back now. They debrief them. When *we* came back, you was on your own. You didn't know anyone on the plane that you came back with. All of a sudden you were home, and everything was different."

"How did you find other veterans?" I ask.

"Down at the VA hospital," he says. "You know everyone down there is a veteran. Sometimes you could see in the newspaper where Vietnam veterans' groups were meeting. Stuff like that. They still have them. They call them support groups."

"But you tried to go to one of those, right, and you didn't like it?"

"A lot of those old boys got there and they were trying to tell who did the worst. If one killed four people, the next killed five. Another killed seven. They were trying to outdo each other. That's all I know how to tell you. I couldn't take it, and I didn't want to go back."

I want to ask my father more.

"Do you think children and families receive all the support they need when veterans return from war, Dad?"

"A lot better than when I came back. Nobody protests the veterans coming back now, or not that I've heard of. No one holds up bad signs and stuff like that, or calls them baby killers anymore. Now everyone blames the government if they're mad. Not the troops. They welcome them back. When I come back, they should have done that. I never did see a welcome home sign. It was BABY KILLER and stuff like that. They'd have signs that read GET OUT OF VIETNAM, VETERANS GO HOME. They'd have signs out that said DOPE HEADS. I never took the first puff of marijuana or took any pills. A lot of them did it, but I didn't."

"What could Mom and I have done differently?" I ask tentatively. "What could we have done to make things better for you—to have better supported you back then?

"You could have took me out back and shot me," he says matter-of-factly. "That would have solved your problems. Put a little poison in my coffee."

He did not answer the question. Not the way I wanted. But I don't want to press him right now. I decide to drop it for the moment and move on.

"What do you think can be done, Dad? For the families of veterans?"

I have to know. I have to find out.

"You can't back up and undo what happened in Vietnam," he says. "No one is being drafted now. That's why they're supporting troops.

It was the college students who didn't want to be drafted who were protesting the war. When they did get a draft notice, they would go to Canada. Then, when we came back from Vietnam, all those ones that went to Canada were pardoned. I think they ought to have took their citizenship away from them if they weren't willing to fight."

His voice is still calm. Strong.

It is still safe here. But he is not answering my question. I will leave it alone.

"I don't understand how those boys could run away like that," he continues. "I was fighting for the flag. I was drafted. Ain't no way I would go to Canada. I didn't protest. I just went."

"What could Mom and I have done to make things easier?" I ask again.

This time he doesn't sidestep the answer.

"Nothing," he says. "It was all my fault. My problems. I just tried to keep it balled up inside of me. When you come out of the military now, they tell you there is help. They tell you to call this number if you have problems. There's help. We didn't have nothing. We didn't know what to do. The VA didn't even want us. You'd sit there all day. That was the government. They don't do it now, but they did it then. They had the impression that if they turned their back on us we'd go away. Lots of those boys went home and shot themselves or got drunk and drove a car off the cliff."

"Did you play your guitar in the war, Dad?" I ask. As much as I've always considered that guitar an extension of my father, I'd never thought of it as being a part of his war experience.

"No, I was out in the field," he says calmly. "There wasn't a chance.

We would come back to the rear for three or four days sometimes. Shows would come through. People would come through and play. I didn't get to play any."

That must have been tough for him, given how much he loved to play and how good he is. But it also seemed odd to think about soldiers taking a break from the war to see these shows, knowing full well that in a few days they'd be fighting for their lives again.

"Did you play your guitar a lot when you got back?"

"I got into it gradually," he says. "I found out that it was helping me. Then I started to play all the time."

"What do you think it is about the guitar that helps you?" I ask. I'd always known that he seemed happiest when he was playing, but I'd never thought of it in terms of being therapeutic.

"It's just soothing. I don't know. It just helps me. It helps me when I play and drive my neighbors wild. I know I'm doing something." He laughs. "That's why I like to go to those churches. The more I look out and see them squirm, the more I like it."

I have to laugh, too. But then I am serious again. "I think that's why I like to write," I say. "Not to make people uncomfortable, but because it soothes me and helps me."

"Gets your mind off stuff," he says. He knows how it is.

"What will you do tomorrow?" I ask.

"I need to burn a brush pile. I was going to do it today, but the wind was blowing. I need to cut more trees, too."

My father mows the lawn several times a week in the spring and summer and mulches the leaves every day in the fall. He likes to stay busy. Like me.

"I bought some more books about Vietnam," I tell him.

"Did you read them?"

"I've read a few pages. I haven't had time yet," I say.

"Them books should have stuff about the protesters in there," he says. "All the LZs, too. The only nurse that was killed was killed in Chu Lai in a hospital. I was in Chu Lai when she got killed. She was working in the hospital there. They shot rockets in. One of them went through the roof and killed her."

"I remember your telling me about the nurse who died," I say. Then, after a pause, "Dad, I have something else to tell you."

"What is it?" he asks, sounding anxious.

"Don't worry, it's good news," I reassure him. "I went to a support group this evening."

"A support group?" he asks, unsure how to take this news. "What kind of support group?"

"It's called Veteran's Heart Georgia," I say. "It's a support group designed to help people who are affected by war. They meet once a month. It's a safe place for people to get together and talk. I just found out about it this morning, and it turned out there was a meeting this evening. There were only eight people in the group, but all of them were either veterans, children of veterans, or therapists. Two of the veterans had been in Vietnam. There was one girl around my age who was the daughter of a Vietnam veteran. Her father doesn't come to the meetings, but she's been going to them for a while. Her name is Katrina." I'm so excited that the words are just spilling out.

It was so liberating to hear people talk so openly about the many wounds of war—both physical and emotional—that I wished I'd known about it sooner. When I decided to go, I hadn't planned to talk at all. I figured I'd just listen and get a feel for the group. But after a few minutes I found myself sharing my story as if I'd known these people for years. I tell my father all of this.

When I'm done, there's a silence on his end. I don't think he has a clue what to say, and neither do I. The magnitude of what I've just shared with him and how far we've come in our relationship in three weeks is staggering.

When he speaks again, it's on a different subject entirely.

"Doctor Presley," my father finally says. "It has a ring to it, doesn't it? I'm the father of a doctor."

He still can't believe it. Neither can I.

"You know what, Christal?" he says kindly.

"What, Dad?"

"I'm glad you got my genes, girl."

His voice is still solid. Steady.

"You know what, Dad?" I say. "I'm really glad, too."

"Write an ad and give it to Mommy," he says. "An ad that we can put in the paper and say that you are a doctor now. I'm really proud of you. I've been telling all those churches about you when I go sing."

"Write up an ad," he says again, in case I missed it the first time. "Mommy will put it in there, okay? Okay, Christal?"

I promise. I can't stop smiling because he's so proud of me.

Journal

I took piano lessons in high school. We could barely afford it, but I begged my mother so much that she finally gave in. I had stumbled upon a radio station that played classical music, and became obsessed with listening to piano concertos. The peaceful music had such a calming effect on me that I wanted to learn to play the piano myself.

Every Monday night for four years I went to Ms. Hart's house to have my lesson. I secretly wished Ms. Hart would adopt me. I felt hurt when she would talk about her two sons. They were older than I was—in college by then.

Ms. Hart was a pianist and a painter. She'd traveled far from our little town in Virginia and had seen people and places that I'd only read about. She could change the way she spoke when she wanted, could speak eloquently or with my own Appalachian dialect. She gave me tons of presents: bags with my name painted on them, pencils with fuzzy balls glued to their ends, and bows for my hair. She made them all herself.

She never missed an opportunity to tell me how wonderful I was, and I soaked it up like a sponge that had been bone-dry for years.

"You are the best piano student I ever had," she said. "You are going to leave this place some day and do something grand. Just wait. You'll see."

I dreamed of leaving, starting over where no one knew me. I could be myself then, find out what that meant and what it looked like.

I almost told Ms. Hart about my father. A thousand times it was on the tip of my tongue. I could trust her. I could feel it. Maybe she could help, point us in the right direction.

But what if she couldn't? What if people came to take him away and he never came back?

I did not tell.

When I left for college I stopped playing, but I stayed in touch with Ms. Hart. In fact, once I left Honaker, she was the only person I kept in contact with. Then, as time passed, and I drifted deeper and deeper into a black hole of depression, I cut off contact with her, too. It was more comfortable to keep people at a distance, to know no one, to never get close, to hide behind a wall and watch the world go on around me.

Reluctantly, during my sophomore year of college, I went home for my aunt's wedding. I was a bridesmaid, sure that the only reason I'd been asked was out of obligation.

I was startled to see Ms. Hart at the rehearsal. My aunt had asked her to play the piano at the wedding. When my old teacher ran over to hug me I wanted to cry and tell her how much I missed her, but once again, I held back. My embrace was stiff and mechanical. I couldn't look at her.

By then, it had become almost physically painful to show affection. If I did, it was pretend—and I was tired of pretending.

I don't know if she noticed my discomfort, but she invited me to lunch and that weekend we went to a little café forty-five minutes outside of town. I insisted that we go out of town because I didn't want people to recognize me. I wanted to stay invisible.

Ms. Hart was anxious to catch up. She said she couldn't wait to find out about all the things that had been going on in my life. What kinds of wonderful things had I been up to these days?

I frowned. If she really wanted to know, I would tell her.

I started with the weekly therapy sessions I was now in, the antidepressants and antianxiety drugs my psychiatrist had prescribed, the lack of sleep, how I didn't go to class because I was so odd and different from everyone else. I told her about my father, how he took his gun to the river. I told her about the sweat pads, how he lost his mind every other day, how I'd finally realized when I got to college that my mother had also been part of the problem, that her behavior toward me was just as inappropriate as his, just in a different way.

By the time I finished, Ms. Hart's eyes brimmed with tears and her face was pale. She was clearly shaken. She reached across the table and placed her hand over mine.

"My God," she said, shaking her head in disbelief. "I didn't know. I'm sorry. I'm so sorry."

I pulled my hand away, and for the rest of the meal we made small talk to break the frequent bouts of silence.

Day Twenty-One

I dread calling my father today. I don't want to break the news. I have cried so much my eyes are swollen shut.

"Daddy," I say quietly, then break into sobs. "Gurpreet and I broke up."

There is a long pause. I cannot stop crying.

"I'm here," he says at last. "I'm right here."

I had seen this coming. There had been problems for quite some time. I just hadn't wanted to acknowledge them. Odd as it may seem, my dogs had always come between us. Gurpreet had never understood my affection for my dogs, Arthur and Duma. It simply wasn't part of his culture. And, in a way, I think he'd been jealous of the attention I gave them. But it was when he came back from Belgium that things came to a head. He asked that dreaded question: "Where is this relationship going?"

It was something I had been thinking about, too, but was scared to ask—probably because I knew the answer already and didn't want to acknowledge it. Gurpreet and I had lived together for months, and it seemed that the next logical step would be to talk about a more serious long-term commitment. That's the way I saw things. But the more I'd gotten to know him, the more I realized how incompatible we really were. Still, I wasn't ready to break up with him. I had grown accustomed to having Gurpreet around. Though I must have known on some level that I was fooling myself, I held on to the hope that maybe, if we just kept going, things would work themselves out.

"You know," he said after asking that fateful question, "I'm never going to marry you as long as you have those dogs. . . . And if we were married, my expectations of you would be higher."

"Those dogs?" Had he really made that statement? And what did he mean about higher expectations? Was I not yet "good enough" to be his wife? It was as if, in that moment, a blindfold had been lifted from my eyes, and I no longer had any doubt—this relationship was over.

Over these past few weeks since I'd been in touch with my father, I had changed—and not in the way Gurpreet would have wanted. I was slowly coming to understand that, all my life, I'd been drawn to men whom I saw as substitute fathers. For many years I'd been so intent on blaming my father for all my relationship problems that I was unable to acknowledge my own patterns. I had been so con- sumed with finding an older man to complete me—and to fill the void left by not having my own father in my life—that I totally failed to consider whether my partner of the moment was a person with whom I was actually comfortable and compatible.

Gurpreet, who was ten years older than I, had filled the bill. Except that now I felt like I had a real father. Substitutes were no longer necessary, and I was no longer willing to change who I was in order to meet someone else's expectations.

Gurpreet left that same evening. Even though I knew that breaking up with him was the right thing to do, I didn't think he'd move out so quickly. I figured it would happen over the course of the next few days, and I'd have that time to deal with the finality of my decision. In fact, I was terribly shaken by how easy it was for him to pack up and go. The only thing that kept me from going totally off the deep end as I had after previous breakups was that this time I now had my dad to turn to.

I honestly don't remember how much I told him that night, but just hearing him say, "I'm here," and knowing that he was present in my life meant everything to me.

"Do you want to speak to Mommy?" my father asks warmly at the end of our conversation.

When he says that, I suddenly realize that it's been a while since I've spoken to her, and I suddenly worry that she'll be upset because I told my father about the breakup rather than her. I fret that I've been so involved in these conversations with my father that she must feel completely left out.

"Yes, let me talk to her," I say, biting my nails.

"I've missed you, Mom," I tell her timidly when she gets on the line. "I'm sorry it's been a few days since we've touched base."

Her voice is surprisingly light and cheery. "That's okay," she says, completely untroubled. "I've missed you, too. But Dad's been telling me about your conversations, and I'm just enjoying seeing you two get to know each other."

My mother's words astonish me. I'd been expecting to apologize to her and instead she seems nothing but pleased for me and my dad. Once again it seems that I've underestimated her.

When my father and I get off the phone, my mother will ask him what we talked about, and he'll tell her about my breakup with Gurpreet. Just three weeks ago, it would have been the other way around. But I know now that her feelings won't be hurt.

Suddenly it seems that, for the first time, I have two parents present and supporting me. Just knowing that gives me all the strength I need.

Journal

College was a whirl of therapists, psychiatrists, booze, and antidepressants. With the exception of my English classes, I signed up for the largest lecture courses I could. Professors rarely took attendance, and as long as I showed up for tests, I could usually scrape by.

For most of my life, I'd known that my severe and constant depression and anxiety were not normal—that I was different from my peers. When I was in high school, I even mustered up the courage to ask my mother if I could see a therapist. It was a brave thing to do because no one I knew went to a therapist, at least that I was aware of. Where we lived, needing therapy was the equivalent of being crazy. Admitting that you needed more than Jesus to solve your problems put you in the same category with crazies who foamed at the mouth and talked gibberish.

My mother said she didn't know any therapists, and even if she did, we didn't have the money to pay for one. Not surprisingly, she encouraged me to talk to God instead.

The fact that I was seeing a therapist and a psychiatrist, taking prescribed sleeping pills, antianxiety meds, and antidepressants while I was in college meant to my mother that I had finally gone off the deep end.

She tried to reel me back in.

"Are you praying about your problems?" she asked every time we spoke on the phone. "Are you going to church? Are you still taking those pills?"

She whispered "those pills" the same way she would whisper "Vietnam."

"We won't tell your father," she said, deciding for both of us. "He couldn't handle it."

My mother still believed that God would save me, but my experience had been different. All my life I'd been told that God's purpose was to help people who were good Christians, and I'd always thought that I was being good. But I certainly wasn't getting any help. In fact, I blamed God for putting me in the place I was, and I believed that He was punishing my entire family. So church was about the last place I'd think of going to get help. Everything I knew about organized religion—and "church" in particular—had led me to believe just the opposite. And God would never do for me what my pills did.

My sleeping pills let me sleep through the night. When I didn't take them, I'd lie awake, my heart racing, a million thoughts flying through my mind like shrapnel from a bomb. But the pills never wore off by the morning, so my mind and my body were always moving in slow motion.

The antianxiety pills, on the other hand, quickened my pulse and made my heart race. I paced my apartment and envisioned myself ricocheting off the walls to expel energy. I didn't take those meds for long.

And then there were the antidepressants that numbed my emotions and slowed my thoughts during the day. They also put me to sleep. So I spent my days sleeping—and my nights sleeping more.

I was so fragile that when I met with my advisor to set up my schedule for my junior year, I broke down and cried. We'd finished organizing my schedule and, as I was getting ready to leave, he asked me, in all innocence, "How are things going?"

"My father hates me," I said, suddenly finding myself sobbing uncontrollably.

His eyes widened as he sat in his swivel chair across from me. "I'm so sorry," he finally mumbled, looking concerned. He did not know what to do with me. Who could blame him? I did not know what to do with myself.

I made an emergency appointment with my therapist that same day, and spent the entire session bawling, mortified that I'd had such a meltdown in front of my advisor, and berating myself for being so out of control.

Day Twenty-Two

"God will work your problems out, honey," my mother says when she answers the phone, referring to my breakup with Gurpreet.

I know she really believes that. I wish I could, too, but her words give me little comfort.

"I appreciate that, Mom," I say, itching to talk to my father.

We say our "I love yous," and she puts him on the phone.

"I am going to take you to the VA hospital here," my father says as soon as he picks up. It's clear that he's been planning this and couldn't wait to tell me. "When you come home for Christmas, we can go down and look around. I want you to go. Will you go?"

"I will," I say. But my heart and my head really aren't in it tonight. Gurpreet's words still sting, and I'm having a hard time getting past the fact that I'd ever thought he'd loved me. Once more I'm sure there's something wrong with *me*.

There is a long silence between us.

"Can I talk to you about something, Dad?" I ask timidly, as if I were a little girl again.

"Sure. What is it? What do you want to talk about?" he says thoughtfully.

The dam explodes. I water my keyboard with my tears. I can't get the words out. It's hard to breathe. "I think . . . I think there's something wrong. Something wrong with me," I manage to gasp.

"Something wrong with you where? What do you mean?" He sounds excited, but not in a good way.

"Something inside me," I say. I am sure of it. There is no doubt. I can't hide it anymore.

"I can't form long-term relationships with . . . men. It's hard to form relationships with anyone. Something is wrong with me." I start picking my scalp and rub my eyes until they're raw. My psoriasis is flaring up with a vengeance.

"Nothing is wrong with you," he says, clearly concerned. "You're a good girl. Please don't cry. You'll get me upset. Please don't cry."

I cannot stop. I don't believe him.

"Do you want to talk to Mommy?" he asks, his voice anxious now.

"No, I want to talk to *you*," I say forcefully.

"Don't try to get close to anyone," he says. "Just be friends with people. Concentrate on your writing. That's what I do with my music."

"But, Dad, I *want* to get close to people. I just can't." I'm crying so hard that I don't know if he can understand me.

"Just be friends," he says, his voice strong and convincing now. "When you get close and something happens, it hurts. Be friends. You'll find someone eventually."

This is not good enough. Something is missing. A piece of me is missing.

"But don't you miss being close with people?" I ask. "How can you not miss that?" I am angry now. This is not normal.

"Yes," he says. "But I've learned not to get too close. When you get like this, write. Write like I play my guitar. It will help you."

This is not what I want to hear either. "But, Dad, I'm afraid I'm going to grow old," I plead, "and the only thing I'll be able to get close to is a piece of paper. Don't you see that? This is not what I want."

"You've got your dogs to take care of. You've got people who will read about our conversations if you write a book. You'll help them," he says. He sounds so certain.

I know my father's trying to help me, but I worry that he doesn't fully understand how much I want and *need* to build relationships with people. "I don't *know* those people, Dad."

"You know lots of people," he insists.

No. I don't.

"Have you ever thought about moving back home? Back closer to us?"

My heart races, and my throat is dry. "No." I say. I will not waver.

"We worry about you, Mommy and me," he says softly. "You should come back home."

No. I can't. I *won't*.

He doesn't understand what he is asking of me. The flashbacks alone would kill me. I have to be in a place where I can stay grounded.

"I'm so proud of you," he says gently.

Another long silence.

"This cat is in my lap. You should see it. I wish you could see it," he says.

I close my eyes, take deep breaths, feel my feet on the floor beneath me. I imagine my father and his cat, the cat twisting this way and that as my father rubs his calloused fingers across its back. We are alike, my father and me. In all the good ways *and* the bad. I pray I haven't hurt him tonight.

It takes awhile for me to calm down, but I do.

I always do.

He gives me time, doesn't push. He understands.

"Are you still there?" he says after a while.

"Yes, Dad," I whisper. "I'm still right here."

"Me, too," he says.

Journal

In college, I was romantically obsessed with my male professors. First there was Dr. Aaron, a short, stout middle-aged man who taught medieval literature. He read Chaucer to us in Middle English, and we sat around in a circle and talked about courtly love in the *Canterbury Tales*. As I closed my eyes and listened to him read, I fell in love with the ebb and flow of the words.

He never came in with a lesson plan. A flaming liberal, his philosophy was to let whatever happened happen and to facilitate class discussions on whatever people felt like discussing that day. He was also a huge Bob Dylan fan and brought his music in so that we could listen to his ballads and compare them to the ballads of medieval times as a way to explore the oral tradition.

I was in love with Dr. Aaron and daydreamed about our being married. He would "complete me." We'd live happily ever after, wake up to the sound of "Make You Feel My Love," and make babies who would love literature and learn to speak Middle English.

The fact that he was thirty years older than me didn't matter.

Then, when things didn't work out with Dr. Aaron, I set my sights on Dr. Koss, an instructor in the education department. He preached against standardized testing in public education and swore he'd pull his daughter out of any public school that forced her to take a test mandated by the federal government.

It never mattered to me that both Dr. Koss and Dr. Aaron were married with children. When I was with them in my fantasies, I was whole. We were happy.

After my crush on Dr. Koss, there was Dr. Fields, Dr. Manus, Dr. Perkins, and Dr. Patel. In my mind, I had relationships with each of them, even though I'd never done anything to get their attention, certainly had never flirted with them or let them know in any way that I was available. On the one hand I would have been mortified to do anything remotely like that; on the other hand I craved affection and longed to be held by a man. I truly thought I would die of loneliness if I didn't eventually have that.

Day Twenty-Three

"We're supposed to get snow here," my father says when I call this evening. "Did Mommy tell you?"

Snow. So we might have a white Christmas. I am pleased. We hardly ever get snow in Atlanta.

"No," I say. "How much?"

"Eight to ten inches," he says.

I remember tubing down the hillside with my neighbors Chris and Amy and how some years the snowdrifts were higher than our trailer. My father would climb to the roof and shovel all the snow off so it wouldn't cave in.

I am surprised that I feel so strong tonight. I am alone in the house with my dogs, but surprisingly, even though it's been only a couple of days since Gurpreet left, I'm actually happy to have the place to myself. I'd thought I would feel as if a piece of myself were missing, but I don't.

Nothing is more important than what I'm doing right now, forming a relationship with my father. It is this that I cling to. It is this that sustains me.

"Tell me some things you like about me," I say to my father. I need to hear this tonight. I need to know. I've always thought of myself as damaged goods. Maybe if he gives me a good reason, I'll be able to like myself better.

"Christal, I just like that you're smart and stuff. You're witty. You got my sense of humor. You're headstrong, too. Like me. You don't let anyone push anything over on you. And you're smart. You're a whole lot smarter than me. God gave me looks, not brains. You know that?" he says, hoping to get a laugh out of me.

I smile. That's the best I can do tonight. Maybe I'll feel more like laughing tomorrow.

"He gave you good looks *and* brains," my father says. "That doesn't seem fair to me. Does it seem fair to you?"

"I don't know," I say. I don't think I'm pretty at all. I don't even acknowledge the compliment when people give it to me.

"Lord, have mercy, ain't no way I could have got a doctorate degree," my father says. "Not in a million years. I never did know English good."

"Tell me what I mean to you," I say. I need to hear this, too. Tonight I am full, yet empty. I have to know what my father thinks of me. I need to brand it in my mind, etch it in my soul so it erases all the bad memories. I need to use it as the foundation I will build on. The foundation must be solid this time. It has been cracked for so long.

He seems shocked that I would ask. "You mean the world to me, buddy," he says. "Why? Didn't you know it? Didn't you know that, Christal?"

I close my eyes. I am alone here, but I am not lonely. My mind is becoming still. There is peace at the end of this tunnel. I am moving in the right direction.

"I just needed to hear it," I say.

Journal

When I was in college, I wrote a short story about my father in one of my creative writing classes. It was poorly written, filled with anger, and contained no concept of time. It was the first time I'd written about my childhood, the first time I'd attempted to share it in public. I changed my name, called it fiction, and passed it out to my classmates without making eye contact with any of them. My voice shook as I read the story aloud. I had to keep stopping to catch my breath.

Everyone was staring, wide-eyed, when I finished. Or did I imagine that?

I waited for the room to explode, but my classmates were silent.

The story was finished, and I could breathe again. A wave of relief washed over my body, as if telling my story—even if I had fictionalized the account—had somehow removed something that had been festering inside me.

"Okay, so we've heard Christal's story," Dr. Fields said gently. "Any comments?"

Rachel Drennon raised her hand. She was a quiet girl who normally left the talking to others. Dr. Fields motioned for her to go ahead and speak.

Rachel cleared her throat. "To be honest, her story pisses me off," she said, her tone obnoxious.

I could tell by the look on my classmates' faces that no one could believe she'd actually said such a thing.

"No offense or anything," she went on, "but the story isn't believable. My father is a Vietnam veteran, and he doesn't act like the guy in that story."

I tried hard not to appear startled. I leaned back in my chair and reminded myself to breathe.

"My dad is a good man," she said. "He has never tried to hurt me or threatened to kill himself. He wouldn't do that."

Dr. Fields was quick to respond. "So, what you're saying, Rachel, is that you didn't find the father in Christal's story believable because it doesn't match your experience with your own father?"

Rachel frowned. "The story gives the impression that all Vietnam veterans are messed up. I don't agree with that," she snapped impatiently.

"But the story doesn't say anything about *all* Vietnam veterans," Dr. Fields pointed out. "Only one."

Rachel crossed her arms. She didn't have a response. No one else said anything either. I convinced myself that they all hated my story. It must have been so bad that no one else could think of anything to say. But just reading the words had been a relief; it somehow lightened my burden. Unfortunately, at the same time, it validated what

I had feared more than anything—that people wouldn't believe it.

Finally, after what seemed like a very long time, one boy raised his hand and said, "I thought the story was powerful . . . especially the way time was twisted and the little girl kept having flashbacks."

Others nodded.

"It was real to me," a girl named Cyndi said. "I could really see the girl hiding in that closet."

I didn't look at Rachel. It wasn't supposed to matter what she thought, but it did. It mattered what they all thought, because the story was real. I was relieved to hear positive feedback from at least two of my classmates, though it didn't entirely offset how offended I was by Rachel's comments.

"I want to tell you all something," Dr. Fields said before we left class that day.

He always made it a point to end class with some words of wisdom. Sometimes they were stories about his youth. Other times, they were quotes on which he wanted us to reflect. Today he looked somber.

"I lived through the Vietnam War," he said. "I never went, but I lived through it—right here in the U.S."

The room was still, the fluorescent lights humming overhead.

"Vietnam was no joke," he said. He shook his head back and forth. "Maybe you had to have been there to walk in our shoes. All of America was at war with itself. It didn't matter if you went to Vietnam or not. You took a side. The whole country was divided. Martin Luther King Jr. was killed during that time. Bobby Kennedy was assassinated. It was the end of the goddamn world as we knew it, and we've never gotten over it."

His eyes were red. He shook his head again. "I just wanted you to know that," he said.

Even though I wasn't yet ready to apply what he had said to my father's situation, it was disturbing to me that someone who hadn't even fought in the war could have such an emotional reaction. I also wondered then—and to this day—whether Dr. Fields knew, or suspected, that my story wasn't fiction at all.

Day Twenty-Four

"We got a big snow here," my dad says enthusiastically. "Probably sixteen inches. We're stranded."

I miss being stranded in the snow. That never happens here in Atlanta.

When I was young and living in the mountains of Virginia, the best feeling of all was staying in my pajamas all morning when school was canceled, putting on my snowsuit after lunch, and then trekking through the fields with my neighbors Chris and Amy. My mother made soup for lunch. Ramen noodles. I ate the seasoning right from the tiny foil packet when she wasn't looking, then emptied the rest into the soup when it came to a boil. Amy and I had a noodle fight once. For months, my mother found noodles all over the house.

I am starting to remember things I thought I'd lost.

I am going to have a white Christmas this year—if I can get back there.

"It's still coming down," my father says. "Supposed to come down until Wednesday. Aren't you coming home next week?"

I am.

I'm surprised by how good I feel today, how happy I am.

You are not supposed to be this okay. You broke up with your boyfriend three days ago, remember? a voice inside me says.

I shrug her off. I like what is happening to me.

I think about my father a lot now. He loves me. He thinks I'm pretty. He says I'm smart. This is all that matters.

I hear his voice again and again. "You mean the world to me," he says.

I really don't know how to respond to that. It's too emotional for me right now. So I retreat to my fallback position and ask him something about the war.

"Tell me more about what it means to be a radio carrier, Dad. I know you did that in the war. I want to know more about it," I say. I want to see if he'll talk about the war tonight.

"For about six months, I carried a radio," he says without hesitation. "It was a radio that you talk through like a telephone. You have numbers, and you call in. You've got call signs—like Bravo One or Alpha One—that you call into. It was a PRC-Twenty-Five radio. It was big, probably weighed twenty or twenty-five pounds with the battery. It had a little antenna on it. You could change the little one out and put a great big one on. The bigger antenna would mean you could call out to a farther range."

"What was your job as radio carrier?"

"When we found the enemy, I would call in for support. If we ran out of ammo, I would call in for more. If we needed food, I'd call. Things like that. I was in charge of calling." This sounds like a tremendous amount of responsibility.

I tell my father that I had lunch with Katrina today, the woman I had met at my first Veteran's Heart Georgia meeting.

"Tell me about it." He's really interested.

Where do I begin?

"What does she do?" he wants to know.

"She's a scientist. She also teaches chemistry," I tell him.

"Has she got it, too? Symptoms of PTSD, too? Like you?" His voice is shaky now. My stomach turns. Please God, do not let this cause him to have an episode. He's seemed so strong lately. The last thing I want to do is trigger a setback.

"Yes," I say timidly, holding my breath.

"What did the two of you talk about?" he asks.

I'm not ready to give him all of the details. Maybe I never will. I tell him that Katrina and I talked about our symptoms and about being daughters of Vietnam veterans. General information only. He does not ask for more.

The truth is, I am bursting at the seams after talking to Katrina. Finally, I have met someone who understands me. It's the first time I have talked face to-face with another daughter of a Vietnam veteran with PTSD. Katrina has the same social anxiety, depression meshed with anger, and recurrent nightmares. Like me. She was odd growing up and never fit in. She can be a hermit, revels in being alone. It's a challenge for her to be social and hard for her to form relationships. Like me. We talked for hours in the coffee shop, telling each other our entire life stories though it was only the second time we'd met.

It was so easy. I could never have imagined how light I'd feel after talking to a complete stranger. It was as if we knew each other without knowing each other at all. It is the same with war veterans, the reason my father wears military jackets, belt buckles, and caps embroidered with VIETNAM VETERAN. It is important to find one another. I am starting to understand this now.

Her whole life, Katrina had felt she was drifting, just barely getting through. But things are different now. These days, she is using yoga and massage to control her symptoms. It's working. She is attending Veteran's Heart Georgia for support and finding other people who can relate to her story. Like me.

My father's voice brings me back to the present. "If you look in that Vietnam encyclopedia, you may be able to see those radios," he says. "There might be a picture in there. You had to be on a certain frequency, and they'd change those frequencies all the time. There were two little knobs on the radio where you changed the frequency. They'd send orders out on the helicopter and write on a little piece of paper what frequency they wanted us to be on. Like sometimes at night at twenty-four hundred hours or so, they would tell you the frequency needed to be changed to thirty-five seventy. I'd have to get up at midnight and change the frequency. Otherwise, the enemy would catch on to what frequency we were on. They'd hear where we were and where our supplies were supposed to be dropped. We had to keep them confused."

"How did you know who you were calling or who was calling you? Did you use names?" I ask.

"No, no names. I was Alpha-Three. That means my whole squad was Alpha-Three. That means I was in the third platoon, Company A. Do you understand?"

I'm not sure. It seems complicated.

"Company B was Bravo. Company C was Charlie. Company D was Delta. They went A through Z like that. I used to know all of them, but I've forgot now."

He tries to recite them and gets all the way to T.

"Lord, I wish I could remember them all," he says. "I think I'm telling you right about Alpha-Three and the third platoon. It's hard to remember those things now. When you get off the phone, look in that book and find the radio," he instructs, and I agree.

I need to ask him a serious question now. I hope he will be okay with it.

"Dad, when you have bad dreams, what do you dream about?" I ask tentatively.

"I dream about being back over there. Especially when I get depressed. Then I have the dreams. Or when there's a thunderstorm at night, I have the dreams."

"Do you still have those dreams?" I ask.

"Yes, I do."

I do not tell him about *my* dreams of the war. I don't want to get him upset.

"What do you do after you have one?" I ask. I need to know this for myself, too.

"I don't do nothing," he says. "I just can't go back to sleep. I just have to let it wear off." He pauses. "You're coming home on Wednesday, right?" he asks again. He has had enough of the war tonight.

"Right," I tell him.

"Mommy sent a picture of the cabin on the computer," he says. "Did you get it?"

I did. The cabin my father has been building for years is almost complete. My parents have decorated it for Christmas.

"Are you bringing your dogs?"

"Yes, both of them," I say. "What do you look forward to most about me coming home for Christmas?" I ask.

"I just want to see you," he says. "I never get to see you. I want to spend some time with you."

I smile. It feels good to be wanted.

"I want to see you too, Dad," I say.

"Don't forget to look for that radio in the book," he says. "And bring a lot of money when you come. You can take me out to eat."

I laugh. "Okay. I'll do that. And tell Mom I'm sending her my love."

Journal

I don't remember for sure what happened the time I had what I still think of as a nervous breakdown. I had loaded Cruiser and Zeus, the two Afghan hounds I had back then, into the back of the car and driven to my parents that night. I must have been a junior in college. I don't know why I was going back, and I don't remember how long I planned to stay.

My father was in the driveway when I arrived. There was something in his hands. A plate of biscuits. It was dark outside, but I could see him under the porch light.

He'd been on his way to the back of the house to give the biscuits to his German shepherd mix, Lucky. She was in a chain-link kennel with her own doghouse. The dogs I had grown up with, Smokey and Rusty, had been dead for years.

My father frowned when I arrived that night.

Or did he smile?

I pulled into the yard and turned the car off. When I opened the door, Cruiser and Zeus shot out of the car like bullets. He let out a yell, twisted his body to get away from them, lifted the plate of biscuits over his head.

It happened in slow motion. He raised his leg and kicked them.

Or did he just raise his leg? Did I *think* he was going to kick them?

Did my mind play tricks on me and create something that never happened? Did I see what I wanted to see?

"I hate you!" I screamed at my father. "Do you hear me? I hate you!"

I couldn't breathe. My chest was tight. Something inside me was going to rupture.

My father stood speechless, his mouth agape.

I never made it into the house that night. I don't know how I drove the three hours back to my apartment, but I did.

Then, huddled on the floor, I cried until I vomited, screaming until I was sure someone would call the police, pressed my face into the carpet, and pounded my fists against the floor. My dogs sat on the sofa and watched, terrified.

Day Twenty-Five

My father thinks he might have shingles. He is headed to the VA hospital tomorrow morning to see for sure, and as long as the roads are clear enough my mother is going along.

"If you want some, I'll pick them out and give them to you," he says with laughter in his voice.

I find this very funny. "No, thanks," I chuckle.

They're on his head—little pustules that itch and burn. It sounds like what I have, but mine are not shingles, even though they are stress-related. I've had them since I was a teenager. "Psoriasis," the doctors say. Steroids don't work. Neither do antibiotics. Moisturizers make the problem worse. I've been given special shampoos, oils, and creams. They don't go away. The sores ooze and bleed. If I'm really nervous, they spread to my ears. They come and go depending on how anxious I am on any given day. Mostly, they stay.

My mother blames my scalp condition on my father's exposure to Agent Orange. I've recently read stories of other veterans' children who also have skin problems. Many mention immune disorders. I have even heard of birth defects like Malorie Brumfield's. As with PTSD, it seems that the effects of Agent Orange do not end with the veterans themselves.

"Tell me about Gary Brumfield and his daughter, Malorie," I say to my father tonight. I want to hear this story again because I haven't heard it in years, and because I'm spending a lot of time these days thinking about the possible connections between the health issues of Vietnam veterans and those of their sons and daughters.

Malorie and I began kindergarten together. She was so small, fragile, like a tiny doll. I could see her veins right through her skin. It was scary to look at her, and when we played together I was always afraid she would break.

Gary Brumfield was a Vietnam veteran like my father and had been exposed to Agent Orange in the war. When Malorie was born, she was not expected to survive. Her heart had only three chambers. When we were in first grade, she had open-heart surgery. Our class wrote letters to her in the hospital. She survived the surgery, but she didn't grow or develop normally. At seventeen, her chest filled with fluid. She was in and out of the hospital to get it drained. The doctors at the University of Virginia Hospital finally performed a heart transplant. They said it was the only way she'd live.

She didn't. I was in college when Malorie died. Her body was not strong enough, even with the new heart. At least that's what I heard.

Even though I'd always known how sick she was, her death came as a shock. We'd all thought the heart transplant would finally make her well, and she was making plans for the future. She wanted to be a teacher. She wanted to get married and start a family of her own. It made me sad to think that now she'd never get to do any of that.

"Gary said he knew her heart condition was from that Agent Orange," my father said. "No one believed him then. But now the government says that Agent Orange can cause birth defects. Like the one she had."

"Do you know anything else about Gary?"

"He died of cancer," my father said. "It was a few years after Malorie. The kind of cancer he had was caused by Agent Orange, too."

Agent Orange. How I hate those words.

Lately I have been thinking a lot about Pat Brumfield, Malorie's mother. The war took her family. She survived. I suppose she's still in Honaker, doing her photography and teaching school.

I say a silent prayer for Pat Brumfield's well-being.

"What do you think happens to people after they die, Dad?" I ask.

"They go to heaven or hell," he says. "Why? You don't believe that?"

"I don't know," I say truthfully.

That kind of thinking seems so primitive to me now. Maybe this world is our heaven or hell. Maybe we create our own realities through the choices we make.

"That's where they go, to one or the other," he says. He is sure of himself. "When I die, I'm going to stay in the attic and haunt Mommy. She'll probably be married six months after that. She'll find herself another old man. What do you think?" He laughs.

"No, Dad, she won't."

"I'm the best of the best," he says. "She'll never find anyone like me. What do you think?"

I don't say anything. I'm still thinking about the Brumfield family and heaven and hell.

"It's bad that I have to brag on myself, Christal," he says lightly. He is looking for something validating from me. He wants me to talk about him.

I try to focus on my father. "Do you want me to brag on you more?" I ask.

He laughs. "Yes," he says. "I like to hear it."

This is not natural for me, but I want to do it. He's been telling me how proud he is of me, and I want to give him something in return. "I think you have a great sense of humor and you're a talented musician. I think you really love Mommy and me," I say, and as I say the words, I realize that I truly mean them.

"I do," he says, not kidding anymore. "You are my pride and joy. You would not believe how much I love you. I tell Mommy I love her every day." He pauses. "She says she's just waiting until I die. Then she'll find someone else." Now he's trying to be funny again.

I smile. "Stop it, Dad. She wouldn't do that."

"Yes, she would," he says, chuckling. He is cracking himself up. I love to hear my father laugh.

"She goes to the VA to find prospects," he says. "She hunts them down while I'm in the office. That's the only reason she goes with me."

He is laughing hard now, snorting through his nose.

I start laughing also, and it's suddenly hard for me to breathe, I'm laughing so hard. I don't know why this is so funny, but it is. Imagining my sweet mother—so shy she barely talks to men—prowling around the VA hospital is too much.

"It's good to laugh like this, Dad," I say, relieved that my father has helped me shake my gloomy mood.

"I like it, too," he says.

Journal

"Are you sitting down? Are you still in bed?" my mother asked when I answered the phone. This was ten years ago, my senior year in college.

It was 7:00 AM on a Sunday morning. *Of course I'm still in bed,* I wanted to say.

There was a long pause.

Then I realized something was wrong because she didn't ask me right away if I'm going to church. She didn't remind me that she loves me or ask me when I'm coming home. I sensed something was different that morning.

"Are you sitting down?" she asked again, her voice cracking.

She was crying.

I imagined her sitting alone in her rocking chair in her bedroom, her knees curled into her chest as she rocked back and forth. Her Bible would be on the nightstand behind her.

"I'm sitting down," I replied as I sat up in my bed and pressed my own knees into my chest. I thought if I could make myself small enough, maybe I would disappear and wouldn't have to hear what was coming next.

My father. I knew something had happened before she said the words. I'd waited my whole life to hear it and hoped I never would:

Your father has gone to the river, I expected her to say. *This time he didn't come back.* This would be her code for my father finally going through with it, taking his gun to the river and ending it all for good.

I braced myself. It was hard to breathe. I couldn't let her hear me cry.

"It's your father," she said.

I gasped for air and slid off the bed and onto the floor. If I held my breath long enough, I could make myself pass out and make it all go away.

She sobbed as she tried to speak. I could only understand a few words.

"Doctors . . . your father . . . Agent Orange . . . tumor . . . lung . . . can't wait . . . home . . . please . . . come home . . ."

He didn't go to the river. I could breathe again. But something else has happened.

"Please come home," my mother whimpered between sobs. "Come home, Christal," she begged, her voice wobbling.

I didn't say anything. Her words were whirling in my head.

I sat on the floor, telephone receiver pressed to my ear, and counted the tiles in the ceiling, then the ridges on the bedroom curtains.

My silence was code. She knew I would come.

Day Twenty-Six

"I do have shingles," my father says. He had been at the VA hospital for most of the day.

"What are they going to do for you?" I ask.

"They say I have six months to live. If I'm still here then, they'll do something." He laughs, then gets more serious. "They gave me some pills and ointment. Are you still coming home on Wednesday?"

"Yes." I can't believe it. Four days from now, I'll be home. "Will there be any snow?" I ask. I've been afraid it will all melt before I get there.

"It'll be here," my father says. "We got all kinds of snow. The road crews have scraped and salted all the highways already, so they're clear, but there's still snow all over the ground. You can take some back with you. I'll put it in a bag. You can show them down there what snow looks like."

I can't talk long tonight. I am going to a Christmas dinner party at my neighbors Mary and Elizabeth's house. Mary is the one who went with me to the VA hospital. I tell my father this.

"That's good," he says. "Fix me a plate and bring it when you come home. You can do that, can't you? I'll see if Mary can cook."

"What kinds of things will we do for Christmas?" I ask my father.

"Whatever you want to do," he says.

I want my father to open presents with us this year, and I want him to spend time with me. I want us to watch movies together on the projector he bought. I want to go to the VA hospital with him.

"We can go to Big Daddy's," he says.

"What's that?"

"It's a restaurant in Tazewell," he says. "It's a little country restaurant way back in the mountains. They've got a big buffet or you can order off the menu. Maybe Mommy will pay for it."

"I got my locks changed today," I tell my father.

It's really set in. Gurpreet and I are over. Yet I feel full, not empty.

"What should I look for in a man?" I ask my father.

"Christal, I don't know if they make them like me anymore. That's a thing of the past."

"Seriously, Dad. Come on."

Obviously I need advice, since the choices I'd been making were never the right ones. Not that I am looking. I just want to know, and for the first time that I can remember I truly value his opinion.

"Play hard to get," he says.

"What does that mean?"

"That means don't be interested in them. If one of them looks at you, look at him cross-eyed."

I'm not sure his plan will work. It might have the opposite effect.

"What else?" I ask.

"Look for one that has a lot of money," he says, laughing.

Been there, done that, I think. "What else?" I want to know.

He gets more serious now. "Make sure he can play a guitar good or that he's interested in something, that he has a hobby," my father says. "That's important."

I'm glad we're getting somewhere.

"Find you someone that will take you to church," he says. "Is that good advice?"

"I guess so."

I'm not sure about church, but I like the idea of spiritual awareness.

"How should a man treat me?" I ask. When I think about how I've been treated by men in the past, I realize that I've had pretty low expectations. It's frightening to think how little I valued myself.

"He should open doors for you, stuff like that," my father says seriously. "He should treat you like a lady, never ask you to pay for food or things. He should be good to you. That's all I know."

"What if I'm smarter than he is?"

"You are always going to be smarter," he says. "No way you'd find one smarter than you. You won't."

We both chuckle, but he is dead serious and that is the funniest part.

"You won't," he says.

"Make sure you get a prenatal agreement," he says.

I burst out laughing. He means "prenuptial," but I don't correct him.

"Don't you let a man take your house from you," he says. "What's yours is yours."

I promise him I won't.

"If you find someone like me, I want to meet him," my father says.

So do I. There is silence for a long time between us.

"You should see little Duma," I tell my father. "He is so cute. When he gets cold, he sprawls out on top of the heat vent in the floor."

"You should see this cat," he says. "Avery loves to hear me play the guitar. When I start playing, he runs in here to listen."

I can't wait to see the cat listening to my father in person.

Journal

When my mother asked me to come for my father's lung surgery, I didn't want to leave Blacksburg, my university town. There, the mountains rolled from one to another in predictable patterns. There were roads built around those mountains and broad valleys between them. There were businesses there, nice restaurants, and different kinds of people from all over the world. I didn't feel so cramped or closed in there. Also, in Blacksburg I could shut myself up in my apartment for days, ditch class and life if I was in the mood, and stop believing in God if I wanted to. It was a place where I could drink until I could not remember my name and write poetry on the bathroom floor—all if I wanted to.

The mountains in the town where my parents lived were jagged; most of the valleys were so small that nothing could fit between them. Houses were built on ledges, and driveways were steep and made of dirt. Rock was blasted and earth cut to make way for roads.

There was David's Grocery, Honaker Florist, and a gas station downtown. The people were white for miles. The mist that rose above those mountains was gray, as if still tinted by the coal mines that had shut down long ago.

But the real reason I didn't want to go wasn't the smallness of the town or the claustrophobic valleys; it was because of the things I knew I'd remember. Whenever I drove those twisted roads, the jagged mountains would creep up on me, catch me off guard, and the things I had tried so hard not to remember would descend upon me. There would be no stopping them.

It was already happening. But I knew I had to go.

Day Twenty-Seven

"**D**id you hear from Ralph Stanley?" I ask my father this evening.

He had just sent the famous musician some songs he had written in hopes that Stanley would record them.

"Ralph Stanley asked me to play with him once," my father had always said. He told anyone who would listen. It was his claim to fame.

"I haven't heard from old Ralph," my father replies. "I tried to call him, but only his daughter was there. He is listed right there in the phonebook, you know. She said he was out on the road, at the Grand Ole Opry, she thought. I left a message for her to give to him. He'll either like the songs I sent him or he won't. It don't matter much to me."

I don't believe him. Of course it matters.

"I've seen Ralph and his family at Cracker Barrel several times," my father says. "I've sat right down next to him."

This makes me excited. "What did he say? Did you talk to him?"

"No," he says. "People don't want to be bothered like that when they're eating. . . . My songs may not be good enough for him to record," he continues. "Probably ain't. He'll have to be the one that decides. It's kind of like food, I guess. People like different kinds of foods. Maybe he won't like my kind."

"But he did once," I remind my father. "Why didn't you reschedule the night the blizzard came? What if you missed a golden opportunity?"

"I just didn't," he says. It is as simple as that.

Is it really? I am not convinced.

"I went to Bristol today to get my guitar fixed," he says. "It was busted. That boy down there who fixed it can really play a guitar," he says. "He says he plays in bands, travels all over the place."

That was my father's dream at one time, to travel the country and sing, to make it in Nashville.

"Is he better than you, Dad?"

"Lord, yes."

I am shocked. I have never heard my father admit that anyone was better than him at anything, especially at playing the guitar.

"Dad, Mom said you told her a story about being in the grocery store one time when you heard a loud noise and knocked over the tomatoes. Will you tell me that story?"

I wait anxiously for his response.

"I thought I told it to you," he says.

"No, you didn't."

"At Food City, around Easter, a woman was blowing up balloons. It was over on the side where the fruits and vegetables were. I saw her when I walked through the door. I picked up what I needed and forgot she was there. When I got beside her, one of those balloons busted. I almost tore the whole shelf of tomatoes down. I thought it was a gun that went off. It embarrassed me. I hit the floor. You just do it before you think. I thought it was a gun," he says matter-of-factly.

"You had to be alert all the time like that in the war," I say. "It would happen to anyone."

I remember the times as a child when I would accidentally drop a cup or a plate. The sound sent him into panic mode. In an instant, his eyes would become huge and bloodshot, his pupils dilated as big as marbles. He'd jump several feet in the air from a seated position in reaction to the noise. After that he'd fly off the handle, scream at me, and chase me around the house. I was constantly terrified that I'd do something to set him off.

But I want him to know I understand now that he is not to blame.

"When you've been in the war and you've got PTSD like me, any loud noise, you just jump. You can't get out of it. Whenever you hear a noise, you either jump three feet in the air because it scares the life out of you, or you hit the ground because you go into war mode and try to protect yourself. You do it automatically. You don't think about it. It's like hitting the brake on a car. When you're going down the road, you brake and let up without thinking about it. You've done it so long it's like breathing. You don't think."

"I'm really sorry for that, Dad," I say gently. "I can't even imagine what it's like to have to deal with that day after day. I wish there was something I could do to make it better." I pause. "Do you think the war affected your relationship with Mom?"

"Big time," he says. "You ain't close. You try to get off to yourself. Mommy probably didn't like that."

But she understood it, I want to say. She understood it long before I did.

"How do you think the war affected your relationship with me, Dad?" I am calm when I ask this question. I do not pick my scalp or bite my nails.

"Probably the same way," he says. "I never saw you. I never spent time with you. Plus I worked all the time back before I got disabled. I worked ten or eleven hours a day, was gone thirteen or fourteen hours a day. I worked on Saturdays, too. Then after that, I'd mow grass when I got home. I'd work all the time, mow grass all the time, way into the night. I'd do it day after day. It was hard to get close."

"But I can understand now why you did all that, Dad," I say. "I didn't then, but I do now."

And things are different now. We have come so far. I smile when I think about it.

"You should try to call Ralph Stanley again, Dad," I say. I want to see my father's dream come true.

"No, I won't force myself on him," he says. "Besides, I'm too old now to play with him."

Now, *that* is really funny. "Come on, Dad. That's ridiculous. He's a hundred years old. Well, maybe eighty or ninety. You're only sixty." I wait for a moment, then ask, "Who do you think is the best guitar player of all time?" I expect him to say he is, the way he always had before.

"Chet Atkins," he says.

My father is becoming more humble.

"Why?" I want to know. I've never heard of Chet Atkins.

"He's just a good guitar player, Christal. He can do stuff no one else can do."

"What kind of stuff?" I want to know more about this. I'm curious to look up this Chet Atkins to see why my father thinks he's so great.

"He can just play. He's just good. The best of the best," my father says. "He's dead now."

"When did he die?" I ask.

"A few years ago," he says. "He had a tumor on his brain that killed him."

There is silence between us.

"What will you do tomorrow?" I ask my father, at last.

The cabin he's building is almost finished. There is no grass to mow this time of year, no job to go to, no appointments to go play his guitar.

"I'll burn a brush pile," he says, laughing.

Journal

I was never a stranger to death, illness, hospitals, or funeral homes. I was never protected from the sight of my grandfather's urinal bags, the coal-colored phlegm he spit into a tissue, or the way the room got quiet when people left this world.

In the mountains, sickness and dying were social affairs. These were times to meet and pray, times to tell stories and catch up on gossip, and times to match up unwed singles.

But it was always around somebody else's mother's coffin, somebody else's father's hospital bed. Now it was my father who lay small and still in a hospital bed. His eyes were closed. Tubes ran in and out, up and down, every part of him connected to a machine.

I wanted to vomit, to run away to the farthest corner of the world, to scream my lungs out because this couldn't be. I shut my eyes; I could not look.

"It wasn't cancer," my mother said from the blue chair next to his bed, clutching her Bible tight to her chest. She hadn't left his side for a moment. "Thank God, it wasn't cancer."

The surgeon had removed the mass on my father's lung that his doctor suspected had been caused by Agent Orange—and part of his lung along with it.

My mother's words did not comfort me.

Why wasn't my father moving? The surgery had been over for hours. Why were there so many tubes?

My mother rubbed her fingers along his hand. "Christal's here, Delmer," she said softly. "She came."

My father's eyelids fluttered. For a moment, he was awake. When he saw me standing at the door he smiled, then he closed his eyes again.

Here's what I wish I'd done then. I wish that I'd run over and thrown my arms around him. I wish I'd told him I loved him.

But that's not what happened. God, I wish it were. I'd give anything to go back and change it. In reality, I could not bring myself to touch my father or even to approach his bedside. Instead, I stood motionless in the doorway and stared at him from a distance, terrified. I wondered if this would be the last time I ever saw the man I never knew.

Day Twenty-Eight

My mother answers the phone when I call and tells me that my father is in the field burning brush. He must have heard it ringing because a second later he's there, panting for breath. My mother and I barely have time to say a few words before he grabs the phone out of her hands.

"You can talk to Christal later," he announces sternly. "It's my turn."

She laughs.

"I went to the therapist today," I tell my father. I am comfortable talking to him about this now. It's no longer an admission that something is wrong with me. Now it means that I'm working through things, giving myself the attention I need, that I am worthy. I know I can't continue to let myself be defined by the depression, anxiety, detachment, and hypervigilance I've experienced in the past. They're a part of who I am, but there's much more to me than that.

My father's voice is calm. "What did the therapist tell you?" he asks.

I grin. "She said I was going crazy," I joke. It's the sort of thing he would say.

He laughs. "Well, we all knew that."

"She said I'm doing well," I say proudly. "I've made a lot of progress these past four weeks."

"We're thinking of going back over to Vietnam and winning this time," he says, changing the subject.

"Who is *we*?" I ask.

"All of us potbellied, old soldiers," he says, then laughs.

"Do you think you'll ever go back, Dad?" I ask seriously.

"No, I doubt it. I don't want to go back over there," he replies.

"What do you want me to do when I go?" I ask.

"Do what you want," he says. "It's your trip."

"But don't you have any ideas?" I press. I want my father to have a part in the planning of this trip, even if he won't be going. It's a way for me to feel even more connected to him.

"No. Go to Chu Lai. I don't know if anyone knows where those landing bases were anymore." He names all the landing zones (LZs) again, stops on LZ Fat City. "You remember LZ Fat City that I told you about?" he asks. "When we took a shower, we went there. We only took a shower once every month or two. They moved us in clicks. Every click was a thousand meters. If they moved us ten clicks, it was ten thousand meters. When you're out in the field, you keep calling in on the radio. You have to know where you are all the time. That was my job. I'd call in and tell the higher-ups where we were, ask them to send us what we needed. But some of them old boys couldn't read a map," he says. "Sometimes you'd call and ask for artillery and the helicopters would be all over the place trying to get to you. Sometimes they'd end up in Cambodia or Laos."

"That's incredible," I say, shaking my head in disbelief. "The army should at least make sure people can read maps before they drop them into a war zone and expect them to navigate around in it." I pause. "Dad, what do you think about the current wars? The ones in Iraq and Afghanistan."

"I wish they weren't going on," he says. "I can't understand going into Iraq, losing all those people. But I didn't understand the Vietnam War neither."

For a while, he is silent.

"I'm eating buffalo jerky," he says finally.

"*Buffalo* jerky? Where did you get that?" I ask.

"Ordered it from Cabella's. I'm like a cow chewing cud, Christal." He laughs.

"I used to like jerky. Now it hurts my stomach," I tell him.

"This is *buffalo*," he emphasizes. "You were eating the wrong kind."

"Dad, do you think you're receiving the care you need from the VA?" I ask.

"Yes, but they keep cutting back, cutting back, cutting back. I think it's going to get to where they're not going to be able to help the soldiers like they should. They won't have enough money. Every year, they change the rules." When he says that, I can hear the frustration in his voice.

"Tell me more about that." It makes me angry to think that the men who volunteered to fight for our country might not get proper care. It seems to me that's the least the government can do for them.

"Every year Congress votes on what to appropriate—how much money to do this and that. What you have last year you may not have this year."

"That affects the VA hospital?" I feel ignorant. I wish I knew more about these things. That's why I'm asking. "Does the VA change the rules?"

"Years ago, every veteran could use the VA, Christal. Now they can't. If you have a certain amount of money, you can't."

"How much money is it?"

"I don't know. It's *their* rules. If you're like me and you don't have any money, you have nothing to worry about. But your uncle Freddy can't go anymore, and he's a veteran. He and Karen were saving for Hannah's college, and they counted that money against him, told him he couldn't come back because he had too much money saved."

Uncle Freddy is my mom's sister's husband. I had no idea any of this was going on. Why would our government treat veterans like that? It doesn't make sense.

"Lots of veterans don't get free medicine," he continues. "They have copays for medications now. I don't have to pay anything, but some people do. They count pennies. I've watched them count their pennies right in front of me. I feel sorry for them."

"Can you tell me about that couple you met in the VA when you had your lung surgery?" I ask. I'd heard my mother mention this before, but I'd never asked her for details.

"That's Larry Adams. He's dead now. His wife is still alive. Me and Mommy just took her a Christmas present. He died just a month or two after my operation. I went down and sang at his funeral. They lived in Kentucky. A week before he died, his daughter was killed in a car accident. He was really torn up, asked me to come down and be with him. He wanted me to go out and help pick out a gravesite for her. We went to this cemetery and picked out a grave. I pushed him under a pine tree. He was in a wheelchair, had a leg took off at the VA because of sugar. We sat under a pine tree that day and talked about all kinds of things. One week later, he was buried under that pine tree. He's there now."

My throat is dry. I choke back tears.

"What happened to him?"

"He may have had a blood clot," my father says. "His wife said he was eating, looked up, and said he felt funny. Then he closed his eyes and died. I only knew him a couple of months. He's been dead ten years now. His wife still calls here about once a month. She's even been up here a time or two. Me and Mommy's been down there, and she's come up here. We went to Norton once and met her. She's eighty-some years old and can still drive. She had her hip or knee replaced right before Christmas last year."

"Does she get to use the VA services?"

"No, she doesn't get to use the VA. Her husband wasn't declared a hundred percent disabled," he says, "even with his leg took off."

"Is that why Mom gets to go to the VA—because you're a hundred percent disabled?"

"Mommy can't go to the VA. She can go anywhere else, though, and the VA will pay for it. That doesn't seem fair, does it? I was the one that went to war. I think I ought to send Mommy over there and let her fight for a while. I may send her to Afghanistan." He laughs a little.

I don't find this funny.

"What was the farthest away from home you ever went before you got drafted?" I ask.

"Went two places," he says. "I went to Abingdon and Bluefield with my neighbor Joe. Both are about an hour away. Those were the only two places I ever was before I went to the war. We'd get lost every time we went to Abingdon. We would fish there, and sometimes go to take the tobacco Joe's daddy grew to the warehouse."

"Who do you think the VA should take care of?" I ask, jumping back to the previous conversation.

"They should take care of all veterans and their families," he says, "but especially the veterans. Sometimes even the veterans don't even get taken care of."

I am remembering the shingles now. He'll have to go back soon for his follow-up. "When do you have to go back to the VA?"

"January fourth. I told you what I told that nurse, didn't I?"

"No," I say.

"That nurse said shingles come from stress. She wanted to know if I'd had anybody die lately. I said no, but I had my mother-in-law in the car Friday night and got stuck in a snowstorm. I was afraid I'd have to spend all night with her in there. Talk about stress! What do you think about that, Christal?"

My father is cracking himself up.

I smile. "I'm going to tell Mamaw Shortridge what you said, and we'll see what she thinks about it."

He laughs. "Go right ahead."

Journal

In 2000, I left Blacksburg to teach AP English at a high school in Chatham, Virginia. Chatham was a two-hour drive from Blacksburg and almost a five-hour drive from my parents' house. Three hundred miles was the most physical space there'd ever been between my parents and me, and this made me feel more distant from the turmoil back home. I knew I wouldn't feel so guilty about not visiting them, and I hoped the distance would make it easier to start a new life for myself.

I didn't know if I'd have a knack for teaching, but I didn't know what else to do with my English degree. I had always dreamed of becoming a writer, but I didn't think I had anything to write.

As it turns out, teaching grounded me in a way that nothing else ever had. Suddenly I had a purpose. I had people who admired me and valued what I had to say.

My students and I discussed good versus evil in *Beowulf* and how we all have monsters in our lives. Many of them talked about their own monsters and trusted me with that sacred part of themselves. It amazed me how much pain and strength I saw in those kids, who were just a few years younger than me. Many of them seemed to have knowledge beyond their years, the weight of the world on their shoulders. Their eyes looked heavy. I knew those eyes.

It was there in my classroom that I first saw the light in my darkness, that I realized I had a place in the world.

I went to my students' ballgames, their awards dinners, and their families' funerals. Chatham was a low-income area with one of the highest unemployment rates in the state, so when they didn't have the things they needed, like cleats for softball or baseball, or money to buy the books the school said they were required to purchase for my class, I bought them.

I was surprised and gratified to find that they were so interested in what I was teaching that they brought their books into the stands at football games. We'd sit together, ignoring the game on the field below us, and they'd ask me questions about what we'd been studying in class and about the people who'd written the texts we were reading.

"Tell us about Edgar Allen Poe," they'd say. Or about Jonathan Swift or Chinua Achebe. "What do you know about the kind of man Shakespeare was?" they'd ask. "What about Emily Dickinson?"

They brought their journal entries, poems they'd written, and lyrics from their favorite songs to share with me in class. We talked about issues that weighed heavily on their minds: the meaning of life, how to deal with death, the quest for happiness and contentment, and more. I didn't have all the answers and told them that up front. We'd explore these issues together through literature, and learn together in the process. That was our plan.

I barely spoke to my parents during this time. It was better that way. I was still trying to get my life together and I couldn't allow myself to get sucked back into the vortex of those negative emotions. Professionally, I was doing pretty well (I'd even bought a log cabin with five acres of land), but my personal life was still a disaster. I had gone through more boyfriends than I could count in just the last couple of years.

First, there was Jeff, who was twelve years older than me, had a baby, and had been recently separated. It didn't matter to me that he had left his wife and child the night before we met. I needed to be held, to be touched. We were together for two months. Then there was Peter. He was twenty-five years older than me, a professor at the local community college. I drove by his house at odd hours, conned a police officer into running the licenses of the mysterious cars in his driveway, and hunted down the women when I found out who they were. It turned out there were four besides me. I introduced myself to each of them as his girlfriend, even though we'd only been on three dates. At the time, I was so obsessed that it didn't even occur to me that I had become a stalker, but when Peter found out he was appalled and told me that he never wanted to see me again. After Peter, there was David. Then Phillip. Joseph. Edward. A waiter in a Mexican restaurant. There were too many to count. I don't remember all of their names.

• • •

After three years of teaching, I started working toward a PhD in education, which would enable me to teach teachers how to teach. Since I'd never had any actual experience teaching middle school myself, I requested a move and was now teaching eighth-grade language arts. That's when I met Tyler. His mother was the library aide at my new school. She was a warm woman who hardly ever stopped talking. I liked her at once.

"I have a son about your age," she said to me one day. "The two of you should meet."

Tyler and I met later that week, and we were engaged a few months later. Tyler needed someone as badly as I did. It felt good to be needed.

On the day of our wedding, I stood with my father outside the church. It was time for him to walk me down the aisle. I hadn't wanted him to give me away. In fact, I'd fought with my mother about it. He hadn't been there for me when I was growing up, and we barely talked to each other. It didn't make sense to me that a man I didn't know—and didn't even like—should give me away.

My mother cried uncontrollably. How could I do this to the family? How could I turn my back on the very people who'd given me life? She hadn't raised me to be so disrespectful, to dishonor my father.

I finally gave in. The ceremony would be short. Twenty minutes at most. I could handle my father for twenty minutes. To fight it would take more energy, and I didn't have any more energy.

"Please don't do this," my father said that day as we stood outside the church. He looked sad. His voice quivered. "We can leave right now," he said. "I can take you away from here. What if this is a mistake?"

His words twisted my insides into knots. Somewhere deep down I must have known he was right, but at the time I was so angry with him that I didn't want to hear what he had to say.

He reached for my hand. I pushed him away.

A year later, my husband left one morning and didn't come back.

By that evening, my mother was in Chatham, lying on the bed next to me, holding me close. I was crying so hard I hyperventilated, shook, and screamed, a grown daughter now with an aging mother beside her. The next morning, she talked to my father on the phone in hushed tones. My eyes were swollen shut.

"Your father loves you," she said. "He knows you don't have any money. He said if he has to, he'll sell his guitar to pay for your attorney."

Knowing that he would be willing to do that—to part with the thing that was most precious to him in order to help me—made me feel really guilty, but I still wasn't ready to forgive him for what he had put me through as a child.

Day Twenty-Nine

"It's snowing here again," my father says. "There's still a foot of snow on the ground from the last storm, and now there's another inch on top of that."

I wish it would snow here. It might as well, it's been so cold. One of the reasons I moved south was to escape the frigid temperatures of my youth. But last night it was seventeen degrees. It's not supposed to get this cold in Atlanta. Meanwhile, I am so excited I can barely contain myself, so thoughts of the weather pass quickly.

"Dad, do you remember my college roommate Ashanté from Virginia Tech?" I ask. I'm pretty certain he'd met her once when he and my mother came to Blacksburg to visit me. "She said she ran across an old picture of us, and decided to look me up," I tell my father eagerly. "She called me last night."

"Maybe. I might remember a little bit of her," he says hesitantly.

I cannot wait to tell my father this story. "Well, it turns out that Ashanté married a Vietnamese guy named Vien. He lived in South Vietnam as a child."

"I might remember her," he says with a little more certainty.

I have not kept in touch with her or anyone else from college. I'm surprised and amazed that Ashanté called me out of the blue, and dumbstruck by the coincidence of her having married a Vietnamese. Of course, I told her all about the thirty-day project with my father, and about my plan to go to Vietnam. She seemed as excited as I was by the fortuitous chain of events—her having found the picture and deciding to track me down and my having at the same time started to reconnect with my father and planning a trip to her husband's home country. She told me all about how he and his family had to flee the country, and now I couldn't wait to share my information with my father.

"So, Vien and his family left Vietnam when the North Vietnamese took over," I tell him all in a rush. "They couldn't stand the thought of being forced to be communist."

I feel like I know what I'm talking about when I discuss the war now. I've been reading the Vietnam War encyclopedias and studying the other books I've bought. I've read about the reeducation camps that were intended to teach the South Vietnamese how to be communists but actually made them prisoners and slave laborers.

"Vien's family was rich back then," I say, "but they sold everything they had and carved their own boat out of a tree trunk to escape. They sewed their jewelry into their clothes, packed food, and took off. For weeks, they floated at sea. A few times they almost drowned.

When it rained, the boat filled with water and began to sink. They had to constantly pour the water out."

"I remember hearing about things like that," my father says when I stop for breath. He sounds really interested.

"They made it all the way to Hong Kong," I go on. "They were refugees there for a year. Then they managed to get to the United States. Isn't that an incredible story? I've found other stories like it online. People like Vien's family were called 'boat people.'"

"I've heard of those boat people," he says. "I didn't know anything about them, but I've heard of them."

I want to ask my father another question. I am ready. I wonder if he is.

"Dad, what haunts you most about the war?" I ask.

"Why do you want to know?" he asks warily.

"I just do," I say. "You're my father, and I'm an adult now. You can tell me things—if you want."

He hesitates. He isn't sure he wants me to know.

"There was a new boy who came to the platoon," he begins. "He was just a kid. The first time we all met him, he whipped out his wallet and showed us a picture of a baby. It was a tiny little thing—just two months old. He hadn't seen it yet."

I bite my tongue and listen.

"When that boy came, I was getting ready to leave," my father says. "I only had two months left, and then they were shipping me home."

He takes a deep breath, exhales slowly into the receiver.

"If you didn't have much time left on your tour, they put you at the back of the line," he says. "They made the new guys go to the front. They had to trade places with the guys who were finishing their tours."

My father struggles to steady himself.

"They made that boy trade places with me," he says. "They stuck that feller near the front of the line and put me in the back."

There is silence, but this is not the time for questions. My father will continue when he's ready.

"That boy ran up on a booby trap," he says after a while. "Not just him, but several of those fellers up at the front. They didn't know what hit them, didn't see it coming. Here one minute and full of shrapnel the next. Those boys were cut in half."

He pauses, breathing hard now.

"That boy never got to see his baby," my father says. "He had been in basic training when it was born. I lie awake at night and think about that boy—how that should have been me. I don't know why I lived, why things happened like that."

I do not speak.

There are no words.

• • •

I tell my therapist Dr. James this story, and tell her it took everything in me not to pick my scalp raw after hearing it. I wanted to do it. God, I wanted to.

But I didn't.

I picked my pants instead, moved my index finger back and forth, around in circles on my thigh, pressed my fingernail deep into the material. I picked those pants until I had almost worn a hole there.

Dr. James had told me about this technique before, how it may be easier to give up one thing if I replaced it with another. So far, it's working.

It is our last session together. She leans back in her chair and crosses her legs. I don't want my time with her to end.

"Is there anything else you want to talk about?" she asks.

I pull my knees up to my chest and lower my head. "Some days I'm still afraid," I say. "I'm afraid of the future, afraid I like being alone too much, afraid I'll always be socially inept. I am *still* socially inept, you know." I cringe when I say it, and I regret it at once. But what if it's true?

I don't know for sure.

She shakes her head. "That doesn't make sense," she says. "You say you're not social, that you enjoy being alone, yet look at all the things you do. Look at the friends you have. You are changing. Let yourself change. Give yourself permission. . . . You got comfortable being antisocial," she says. "It was a habit. So now you're out of your comfort zone. It's the little girl who wants to go back. She's still scared sometimes, still hides in that closet and holds onto her flashlight. You are not a little girl anymore. You are an adult now."

She looks at me for a long time. I want to break the silence, but I don't. She's right.

Journal

"When I die you'll both be alone if things don't change," my mother said. She was talking about my father and me. I had just moved to Atlanta, having decided to leave Chatham after the divorce. She was visiting.

"He'll die first," I told her. "He's older than you."

My illogical reasoning did not comfort me.

"What will it take for you two to forgive each other?" she asked.

I wasn't interested in forgiveness. At that point I wasn't ready. And, truthfully, I didn't believe that either one of us had what it took to bring that reality to life.

Forgiveness would require me to take a hard look at myself, reexamine the past, and try to remember all the things I'd hidden for so long. It would require me to talk, to open up to my father, to replace the resentment with something bigger than I thought I had inside me.

I spent my evenings reading everything I could get my hands on: *Inferno, The Women of Brewster Place, Robinson Crusoe, Maus, The Jungle, 1984, On the Beach,* the poetry of Nikki Giovanni and Edwin Arlington Robinson, and hundreds more. I read day and night, soaking up words and stories with a vengeance. If my mind was always occupied, I wouldn't have to think about my father.

I didn't realize back then that most of the books I was reading were about survival, about taking what you've been given and molding it into something you can live with.

It was during this time that I also reread *To Kill a Mockingbird*. It had been one of my favorite books since I'd discovered it in high school, but I don't think I understood it back then. Now it took on a different meaning. "You never really understand a person until you consider things from his point of view . . . until you climb in his skin and walk around in it," Atticus tells his daughter, Scout, in the book. Those words hit me hard.

What would it feel like if I could step into my father's skin—if I could walk in his shoes? Would it ever be possible?

My symptoms were similar to his, but our experiences were different. I had not been to war—could not be him, could never wrap my head around that experience. In fact, I'd spent my whole life not knowing him because I hadn't bothered to ask. I wasn't ready to know about the war then. I could not accept the life I'd been given. I did not yet know that by holding my father hostage to his sins I had also made myself a prisoner. I was not ready to forgive.

When I was not absorbed in books, I sat and stared out the window. I wondered who had been the last person to see my father the way he was before the war. It wasn't my mother. She and my father didn't meet until after the war. Even *she* didn't know him back then. And he wasn't close to his parents or his siblings. I wondered if anyone knew the boy he used to be.

Day Thirty

On the way to my parents' house for Christmas, I chew on the sides of my fingernails as I approach John Douglas Wayside in Abingdon, Virginia. This is where the flashbacks usually come, on this dark, windy road that curves up and down a mountain. No sunlight reaches this place. Even on the brightest days, there is only darkness here. I tried to make it home before the sun sets, but I am too late.

The moon is hidden by the thick forest that surrounds me. Trees, heavy with snow, hang over the road, illuminated only by my headlights. There is a foot or more of snow on the ground. I hold my breath, wait, then remember to breathe again.

My whole adult life, I have had flashbacks when I have driven through this place of darkness. I would see my father grab his gun and leave for the river, my arms wrapped so tightly around his legs he would have to shake me free. I would see myself curled into a ball, lying on my bed, my back to the world while he was gone. And I would recall, as if it were real, a dream I'd had in which my father

229

was walking alone at night through the jungles of Vietnam carrying his gun. I was trying to follow him, but it was hard to keep up. He moved quickly through the underbrush, up and down mountains.

I fell behind.

I always fell behind.

I quickened my pace, but I could not catch him.

"Daddy!" I screamed. "Stop! Wait up for me! Don't go!"

In the dream, he always turned. He was standing on top of a hillside looking down into the valley below. I ran as fast as I could. He had heard me!

He waited for a moment, staring into the darkness, then shook his head in disbelief.

"Daddy!" I cried. "It's me!"

He slung his gun over his shoulder and took off into the darkness, like the devil himself was after him.

In the dream, I lost my father. There was no going after him.

Now, I am expecting those flashbacks to come. I brace myself for the jolt and force myself to think of positive things—my father and his guitar, our phone conversations, how he says I am pretty and thinks I'm smart.

I make it to the other side of the mountain. The moon is overhead now, reflecting off the snow and making the whole world glow. I am *here*. I am *home*.

The flashbacks don't come. Instead, I remember something else from a very long time ago.

It is 1983. I am five and in kindergarten. I am an angel in a play, wearing white tights and a light blue dress. On my head is a golden halo made from Christmas tinsel. I do not have wings, but I imagine them. My wings are iridescent, reflecting different colors as the light hits them. I am green, orange, yellow. I am whatever I want to be.

Hand in hand with my classmates on stage, I sing "Silent Night," "We Three Kings," and "Away in a Manger." There is standing room only in our school auditorium.

My father is there with my mother. He is watching, smiling with everything in him from the audience below. He claps after each song and stands at the end when everyone else does. My eyes are only on him.

Afterward, I push through the crowd to find him.

This is before I am scared, before he shakes with anger, before his eyes are wild. Before the war comes to stay. He picks me up that day, holding me close to his chest. I wrap my arms and legs around him, and grin from ear to ear. I am so proud of this man, and I intend to let everyone know that he belongs to me.

This is *my* father—the man who drives with his knees, the one who gives piggyback rides through the woods, the one who built my sandbox, the one who eats my mudpies, the father who hangs his old army hammock in the trees for me to play in.

There was a time before, a time I thought I'd lost.

It's coming back.

• • •

The familiar wind chimes on the porch clink against one another, sounding their approval as my parents and I walk through the snow to the cabin. It is my first night home. We will open presents tonight. We have decided not to wait for Christmas—or even Christmas Eve.

My father has strung lights all over the cabin and arranged my mother's new nativity scene up in the front. She points it all out to me, like a child herself again. I'm thrilled that she seems to be so well. She's a lot more resilient than I usually give her credit for.

"Look what your father did," she says. "He did it all himself."

She beams.

My father lights the candles he has put throughout the cabin and rearranges the presents on the stairs. He stacks them one way, then another, and lines them up in rows.

My mother and I sit and watch him. We are not sure what to do with ourselves. This will take some getting used to for all of us. We will have to learn how to be together this way.

We will.

I know we will.

I smile when I think about how far we have come.

After we open our presents and the night is quiet again, my father reaches inside his jacket and hands me a card. I open it.

There is glitter that flakes off in my hands. Inside I'm amazed to find three hundred-dollar bills. He's signed it LOVE DADDY with a lopsided heart he has drawn himself. *You are my world*, it says. He doesn't want me to forget.

I won't. This time I won't. And I know exactly what I'm going to do with that money. I'm going to use it to buy my own guitar. And I'm going to learn to play it, so that the two of us can play together.

He winks at me and smiles, then pulls another present from behind his chair.

It is a cap. DAUGHTER OF A VIETNAM VETERAN, it reads.

After the Thirty Days

I t is the middle of January, two weeks after Christmas. I have talked to my father every day since my visit. This morning, I awake to find an e-mail from my mother—sent in the middle of the night. "Call your father immediately when you get up," it reads.

Nothing more.

My heart drops. Something is wrong. I grab the phone and dial his number. My hands tremble.

His voice is frantic. He talks fast. "I didn't burn any villages. I didn't kill those people. I know I did some bad things, but I didn't do that. I only watched. Lord, I only watched."

He is breathing hard and pacing back and forth in his room. His eyes are big and wild. I have seen it all before. I do not have to see it now to know.

I don't have time to respond.

"I am going to be taken to jail," he says. "The government will come and take me away for this. They'll try me for war crimes. They'll come and get me. Everyone is going to know."

He has been triggered again. His switch has been flipped. I had hoped it was over; I hoped the war would never come again. But that was never realistic.

Tears flow down my face. I plant my feet flat on the floor and feel the solidness of my body.

"They will get me," he cries, his voice soft and small like a child's.

Breathe. Remember to breathe. I close my eyes.

No one has accused my father of burning villages or of killing anyone. I don't know what he's talking about.

He waits. He needs me to say something. He needs me to make it okay. I fight through the tears.

"It's okay," I say. "I'm here. I'm not going anywhere. I'm with you."

His breathing is a little more regular now. There are some things I need to say to him.

"Dad, when you went away to Vietnam, no one welcomed you home. I'm so sorry for what you went through. I wish I could take that back. I wish I could make it okay. You are the bravest person I know, the bravest person in my world. I'm so sorry that my whole life I didn't see that. I see it now. I see you. I need you to know that. No matter what happened back there, I love you. I'll always love you. Whatever has happened between us in the past, I forgive you. I need you to know that. Whatever I've done, I forgive myself, too."

I say it over and over, my voice getting stronger and stronger.

"I forgive you. I forgive myself. We are going to be okay."

I imagine him moving over to the sofa. He'll sit down, pick up his guitar, and wrap his fingers around the strings. He will play that guitar after we get off the phone. He'll sing his song about Vietnam and pet his cat, Avery. He will feel better for a while. He will have beaten the darkness once more.

He is like that fish I caught when I was a little girl. The one that thrashed and flopped, and sucked frantically for life. The one that never stopped fighting. The one that made it.

Epilogue

The bus turns right off Route 1 in Chu Lai and meanders up a gravel road that cuts through the jungle. The trees are younger here; the jungle is not as thick as other places we have been. Rolling mountains rise in the distance. A long white pole stretches over the road, blocking our way.

The tour bus screeches to a stop, and our guide—a little man named Anh with a permanent smile—jumps out and walks to the guard shed. He waves his hands back and forth as he speaks with the guard who comes out of the shed.

The group of us waits. There are large piles of gravel and yellow bulldozers in the distance. This used to be LZ Bayonet, one of the landing zones at which my father had been stationed. Now it is a rock quarry owned by the government. We might not be able to get in. I'm absolutely stunned—and devastated.

The guard shakes his head no, but Anh continues to speak and wave his hands. When he returns to the bus, he is grinning, showing his crooked teeth. "We get in," he says. He taps our driver on the back, says something we don't understand, and the bus lurches forward. We bounce over potholes and wind up the hillside.

When the bus stops, Anh stands up and grabs the microphone. "Guard almost not let us in. He say he here before, when Americans here. He been keeping guard here for long time. Forty years. Tourists not usually allowed here. This government property now."

My heart pounds. That guard could have seen my father all those years ago.

Anh points to a thin slab of cracked asphalt that's overgrown with weeds and shrubs. It's about fifty yards square and a ditch several feet deep has been dug between it and the road. Thick grass and little yellow flowers line the edges of the ditch.

"Big asphalt was helicopter pad in war," he says. "Has trench dug on one side. Soldiers get in trench and hide. Use like foxholes."

It's hard to catch my breath.

My father was here. He was in this exact place forty years ago.

I close my eyes and think about the conversation I had with him last night. He asked me over and over if I'd really found Bayonet. He promised to be with me in spirit here.

I look all around the bus at my nine new friends, people I feel I've known forever now, who've come from all over the United States to give back, to heal. We have visited treatment centers for disabled children and victims of Agent Orange, volunteered in a home for the elderly, and we will work in orphanages before we leave. We have laughed together, cried together, and prayed together. Each one smiles and acknowledges me.

It is time.

With Skya on one side and her father, John, a Vietnam veteran, on the other, arm in arm we hike the short path to the old helicopter landing pad. Our friends follow with burning incense. It is 90 degrees, 100 percent humidity. Sweat and tears drip from my chin. A jet flies low overhead, the roar of its engine startling in the silence.

We climb a gentle slope to the landing pad and lay the incense in the center. This is all that's left of what used to be one of the largest landing zones in the war.

We gather round in a circle, holding hands and close our eyes.

"This is one of the places where Delmer Presley served," John says. "He probably lived and slept right here, even fought in the mountains behind us."

I imagine my father as a young soldier walking through the jungle with a radio strapped to his back.

Here.

He was right here.

"Today we come to honor Delmer," John's wife, Lindsley, says, "to honor Christal and her mother, Judy Presley. To honor the soldiers that fought and died on both sides. To honor you all. Everyone in this circle has been affected by war. We all carry with us the wounds and memories of that pain. But we don't have to carry it alone anymore."

Her words go right to my heart.

I am not alone.

"We are not all veterans," she says. "But we are all warriors. You are all so brave to have come on this journey. But braver still, it takes a warrior's spirit to heal."

Eyes closed, I let her words resonate deep inside.

It takes a warrior's spirit to heal.

She's right.

After the ceremony, I walk to the edge of the asphalt, scanning the ground for something I can take with me from this place. I spot rivets in uniform patterns near one of the corners.

Tank tracks. They're still here.

I follow the tank tracks to a ledge that drops off into a valley below. As I gaze down into the jungle, I imagine that I am my father. My father, the young man. My father, the soldier. The boy who got on a plane and never came back.

He was right here.

"I have been to Chu Lai," I will tell my father. "I walked on your landing pad at LZ Bayonet. I saw those same mountains, rode down Route 1. I touched the same earth you did."

I think about my fantasy of my father at the beach, running with a Frisbee while my mother waves from the shade of her umbrella. I run behind my father, try to walk in his footsteps, put my feet in the exact places where he has been.

When I look back at the asphalt, there are two green dragonflies circling the ground, their wings beating like little helicopters. There are two smooth boot prints I did not see before, right beside the tank tracks. Their imprints are exactly the distance of a stride a young man would have had.

I smile, take off my shoes, and step inside them.

WHERE WERE YOU?

When I was a young man
I was sent to a far-off country
To fight in a war I still don't understand.
But I was proud to go to serve for my country
In a place they call South Vietnam.
When I got home,
I didn't know about all the demonstrations
They were having at all the airports, towns, and schools.
If you don't mind,
I'd like to ask you a simple question.
When I came home from the war,
Where were you?
Were you waiting at one of the airport terminals
With a big old sign that criticized me?
Or were you somewhere else
Maybe burning up your draft card,
Or hollering "Baby Killer" as I walked down the street?
Now I'll live the rest of my life with all these memories,
But I don't hate you for what you put me through.

Would it make you mad if I ask you a simple question?
When I got home from the war,
Where were you?
Now when I die they'll put me in some
old lonely graveyard.
They'll wrap my casket in the red, white, and blue.
They'll fire a few shots over this old body.
But before I go, could I ask you,
Where were you?
Were you demonstrating on some college campus
With a big old sign that criticized me?
Or were you somewhere else
Maybe setting fire to Old Glory,
Or hollering "Baby Killer" as
I walked down the street?

My father wrote this song in 1970, after he returned home from the Vietnam War, but it took twenty-five years before he played it in public. He told me that he used to play it when he locked himself in his room. I must have heard it, but I wasn't listening.

My Wounds Are Not for You to See

My wounds are not for you to see
Although I wish you knew
Without the grief that hollows me
What holds me back from you

It isn't want of hope or faith
For those I still possess
But muted love that lies too deep
To summon and express

You hear the dreams that end in screams
And tolerate my pain
With fortitude you grace the mood
That I cannot restrain

And that same mood can make me brood
On all that I have lost
My friends, my youth, my naïve truth
O what a dreadful cost

I know that I can weather this
And laugh and love and live

Without regret. And yet
I have not much to give

I need to find the voice I lost
The song I used to sing
I need to feel the warmth of friends
And smell the breath of Spring

I will, I know I will
And we shall share the day
When this chill thaws and I return
And I return to stay

© Frank Ochberg, MD & Gift from Within

This poem was written by Gift from Within's founder, Frank Ochberg. It is based on his experience with combat veterans. Frank served on active duty during the Vietnam era in the U.S. Public Health Service, a branch of the military.

PTSD Resources

Gift from Within is an international nonprofit organization for survivors of trauma and victimization.
http://www.giftfromwithin.org

International Society for Traumatic Stress Studies is an international professional organization that promotes research and dialogue about traumatic stress.
http://www.istss.org

National Center for PTSD, a division of the U.S. Department of Veterans Affairs, promotes research to prevent, understand, and treat PTSD.
http://www.ptsd.va.gov

Sidran Institute is a nonprofit organization that provides resources for people dealing with traumatic stress, including PTSD.
http://www.sidran.org

Soldier's Heart is a nonprofit veterans' initiative focused on creating a network of community-based services to provide healing and reconciliation for veterans, their family members, and their communities.
http://www.soldiersheart.net

United Children of Veterans, founded by Christal Presley, is an online forum for sharing articles and research about PTSD in the children of veterans.
http://www.unitedchildrenofveterans.com

Veterans' Children is an online community that promotes healing and the sharing of stories among sons and daughters of veterans.
http://www.veteranschildren.com

Veterans Crisis Line offers a confidential phone hotline and live online chat that connects veterans and their friends and families with a trained crisis responder.
1-800-273-8355
http://www.veteranscrisisline.net

Acknowledgments

I am grateful to so many people for their support and encouragement during the writing of this book. First, thanks to my editors Allison Janse, Carol Rosenberg, and Judy Kern. Your skillful eyes brought this book to an entirely new level. Thanks to Bob Land for the finishing touches. Thanks to Peter Vegso, Kim Weiss, Kelly Maragni, Lori Golden, Tonya Woodworth, and Larissa Hise Henoch at HCI for your belief in me—and in this message. Thanks to Laurie Bernstein for steering me in the right direction, and to Chuck Adams for his unwavering encouragement. To Eileen Drennen and Michelle Hiskey: You ladies are my rocks. Thanks to Hollis Gillespie and Grant Henry for inspiring me to face my fears—and to Katie Cox, Mary Shaw, Elizabeth Chesnut, Katrina Bergbauer, Carrie Overhiser, Stefany Holmes, Kaye Coker, Ed Tick, Rosemary Rowan, Flavia Gunter, Frances Somerville, and Kimberly Turner for their steadfast cheerleading all during this project. Thank you to Helena Oliviero and Suzanne Van Atten for being among the first to believe in this story, and to Louise Nayer, Lee Smith, Nikki Giovanni, Frank Ochberg, Jessica Handler, and Melody Moezzi for taking time out of your busy schedules to help. Kudos to Rod Howard, Sandy Cox, Ansley Cox, Geneva Booth, and Kay Jo Crowel for your valuable feedback on early drafts. To my friends who traveled with me to Vietnam—John Fisher, Lindsley Field, Skya Richardson, Malissa Landry, Gil Hoel, Mishka Cira, Anh Vu, Tony Luick, Marge McGreevy, and Jeff Luick—I will never forget your empathy and kindness. To my beloved friend Emyl Jenkins Sexton: I only wish you were here to see this moment because it couldn't have happened without you. To my parents: I continue to be awed by your grace, bravery, and trust. And finally, to Brenda Sangster, with love: Thank you for showing up when you did.

About the Author

©Lindsey Lingenfelter

Born and raised in Honaker, Virginia, Christal Presley earned her bachelor's and master's degrees from Virginia Tech, and her PhD from Capella University. She has taught English in public schools in Chatham and Danville, Virginia, and is now an instructional mentor teacher in Atlanta, Georgia. She is the founder of United Children of Veterans (www.unitedchildrenofveterans.com), a website that provides resources about posttraumatic stress disorder (PTSD) in children of war veterans. In her spare time, you can find Christal at home playing with her two dogs, Arthur and Duma, and tending to her garden and her six chickens. To contact Christal, schedule appearances, or learn more about her or this book, visit www.christalpresley.com.